Groups, Teams, and Social Interaction

Groups, Teams, and Social Interaction

THEORIES AND APPLICATIONS

A. PAUL HARE

New York
Westport, Connecticut
London

Copyright Acknowledgments

The author and publisher gratefully acknowledge permission to reprint extracts from the following:

A. Paul Hare, "Intergroup Relations in Israel," *International Journal of Group Tensions*, 19, no. 2 (1989): 117-136. Copyright © 1989 International Organization for the Study of Group Tensions. Reprinted by permission.

A. Paul Hare, "Categories for Exchange Analysis in Small Groups," *Sociological Inquiry*, 49, no. 1 (1979): 57-64. Reprinted by permission of the University of Texas Press.

A. Paul Hare, "Conformity and Creativity in Negotiations," *Israel Social Science Research*, 4, no. 2 (1986): 21-33. Reprinted by permission of *Israel Social Science Research*.

Douglas McGregor, *The Human Side of Enterprise*, copyright © by the McGraw-Hill Book Company, Inc. Reprinted by permission of McGraw-Hill, Inc.

Library of Congress Cataloging-in-Publication Data

Hare, A. Paul (Alexander Paul), 1923-
    Groups, teams, and social interaction : theories and applications
  / A. Paul Hare.
      p.   cm.
    Includes bibliographical references and indexes.
    ISBN 0-275-93890-5 (alk. paper)
    1. Small groups. 2. Social interaction. I. Title.
  HM133.H3594   1992
  302.3'4—dc20   91-28172

British Library Cataloguing in Publication Data is available.

Library of Congress Catalog Card Number: 91-28172
ISBN: 0-275-93890-5

First published in 1992

Praeger Publishers, One Madison Avenue, New York, NY 10010
An imprint of Greenwood Publishing Group, Inc.

Printed in the United States of America

The paper used in this book complies with the
Permanent Paper Standard issued by the National
Information Standards Organization (Z39.48-1984).

10 9 8 7 6 5 4 3 2 1

Contents

Illustrations

FIGURES

TABLES

Preface

As the title of the book suggests, the contents contain some of my ideas about groups, teams, and social interaction; how these can be placed in the context of several theories; and some applications that may be made for the analysis of various kinds of social situations.

The occasion for writing the book was a sabbatical leave from Ben-Gurion University in 1989-1990. The resources, in the form of extensive collections of literature on relevant subjects, were provided by the library of the University of California at San Diego, where I held an appointment as a visiting scholar in the Department of Sociology. The motivation to try once more to integrate the literature on social behavior in small groups came from the fact that, together with my London colleagues Herbert Blumberg, Martin Davies, and Valerie Kent, I had just completed reviewing the social-psychological literature from 1975 through 1988 for *Small Group Research: A Handbook* (1992). That book was a supplement to my earlier *Handbook of Small Group Research* (2nd ed., 1976), which covered the literature from 1898 through 1974.

In each of the previous editions of my *Handbook of Small Group Research* I tried to show how some parts of the literature could be integrated with a single theory, for example, functional analysis. However, it was not until I was asked to give a series of lectures in Polish universities in winter 1989 that I concluded, once again, that it would take several theories, given their present stage of development, to cover the basic processes in small group dynamics. I say "once again" because I first attempted to use a set of theories to focus on the same incidents of behavior in the late 1960s and early 1970s when I worked with a research team on the observation and analysis of nonviolent direct action with a grant from the National Institute of Mental Health. The goal at that time, as it is now, was to show how the four theoretical approaches of functional analysis, dramaturgical analysis, exchange theory, and interaction process analysis, could be used together.

In the 1960s my understanding of these theories was at an early stage. By the time I brought them together in *Creativity in Small Groups* (1982), the development of the theories was further along. I subsequently added more to the dramaturgical perspective, first alone in *Social Interaction as Drama* (1985b) and then with Herbert Blumberg in *Dramaturgical Analysis of Social Interaction* (1988). I also assembled my thoughts about functional analysis in one article (see summary in Chapter 8 of this volume), had further thoughts about dramaturgical analysis (see Chapter 9), and managed to combine aspects of all four perspectives in one category system (see Chapter 12).

Throughout the years since the early 1950s when I worked with Robert Freed Bales at Harvard as a research assistant, I have followed, and sometimes been involved in, the development of his perspective on interaction process analysis from the twelve-category system of observation to the present multilevel system (SYMLOG) based on three dimensions. My review of "new field theory" (1989a) covers research using SYMLOG from 1960 through 1988. Chapter 11 includes an account of some of the more recent additions to this perspective. The case study in Chapter 10 on exchange analysis is taken from my article with Mueller (1979). Although I have continued to review the literature on social exchange, and the combined category system (Chapter 12) includes exchange categories, I have not continued to make separate applications of exchange theory on its own.

It is the custom, on nearing formal retirement from academic life, to collect one's journal articles on various subjects and publish them as a book. Usually they are not edited nor is any special attempt made to show how they relate to one another. However, in the preface, the reader is advised of these facts, acknowledging the sections that may be duplications or represent ideas that are developed further in later pieces. The reader is encouraged to take this opportunity to follow the development of a line of thought. The selections in Part II of this volume have this character, although Chapter 1 is an attempt to show how they might fit together.

Since I have concentrated on the study of groups for so many years, why this sudden interest in teams? There are two reasons: (1) in recent years I have become more involved with the SYMLOG Consulting Group that is introducing Bales's SYMLOG approach for team building and organizational change, primarily in industrial settings, and (2) I was asked to teach a course on "team building" at the United States International University, where I had a part-time teaching position during my sabbatical year. As I began to read the literature on teams and team building, I found that it was published in a totally different set of journals and books than the ones usually included in the more academic social-psychological literature. I noted that this applied literature provided a fresh perspective on a set of problems that I was familiar with primarily through the observation of laboratory groups of university students.

As you will read, I am aware that once a person with an academic background moves off into the applied area, not only is it difficult to keep up with the literature, but also many business clients are more interested in practical results than in elaborate theoretical perspectives. Thus most of the articles and books on team building rely more on practical experience than reviews and integrations of the literature. Since I am rather long on reviews and short on practical experience leading or training groups or teams, my approach to bridging the gap between theory and practice is clearly from the academic side of the chasm. Hopefully, I will have an opportunity to continue this line of activity. In that case, this book is only a progress report.

You will find that I present only about five "big ideas" in this volume. These five topics were chosen because they were found in most of the applied texts on team building and might usefully be placed in the context of the literature on social interaction in groups.

1. It takes several theories, at their present stage of development, to cover the social-psychological space.
2. Types of groups, teams, and crews can be distinguished if one considers their primary function and type of organization.
3. Groups and teams pass through identifiable phases, both in solving problems and in overall development, and the same intervention or activity may be appropriate or inappropriate according to the phase.
4. Levels of creativity in problem solving can be identified, and many of the tasks suggested for team building make it impossible to have experience at the highest levels.
5. The activity included in books on team building—and indeed in many forms of negotiation—under the heading "conflict resolution," is simply the introduction of the process of reaching group decisions by consensus to groups and teams that were not effective in using the process on the first round.

If you have already reached these conclusions on your own, then this book may simply provide more support for your analysis. If you remain to be convinced, then it is my hope that the present review will at least show you how I reached these conclusions.

Acknowledgments

Finding the time, energy, and ideal situation for writing this book would not have been possible without the support of Ben-Gurion University of the Negev in Israel for a sabbatical year in the United States. For providing an affiliation with the Sociology Department of the University of California at San Diego I have Professor Joseph Gusfield to thank. Joe also uses a dramaturgical perspective for the analysis of social behavior and is thus aware of the marked influence of the setting on social interaction. Professor Roland Tharp, while he was Dean of the School of Human Behavior at the United States International University, suggested that I teach a graduate course on "team building." This provided an incentive to read the team building literature, which was new to me, and to write a first draft of the present book as a set of notes for the students in the course. Feedback from the students indicated that the topics covered in the course were important for persons who planned to be organizational consultants.

The idea that I should once more attempt to show the relationship between the various theories with which I had been working was the result of a series of lectures that I was asked to give at three Polish universities in November 1989. For this opportunity I thank Professor Jacek Szmatka of the Jagiellonian University in Krakow. For bringing me up to date on the social-psychological literature on small groups I am indebted to Herbert Blumberg, Martin Davies, and Valerie Kent, of Goldsmiths College, London, who joined me in the review of the literature that resulted in our handbook on small group research. Over the years Dean Peabody always has been ready to discuss social-psychological issues and to give me the benefit of his encyclopedic knowledge of psychology and many fields and periods of history.

On the applied side, Bob Koenigs and Margaret Cowen, directors of the SYMLOG Consulting Group, made it possible for me to participate in

several of their consulting activities and certification workshops for consultants, providing a window to view the world of team building. Freed Bales,
when he was not busy writing additional programs for group analysis for
the SYMLOG Consulting Group, was a continual source of encouragement
in my attempts to bring various theoretical perspectives together in an
integrated theory.

Several persons read versions of the manuscript and gave general reactions. For detailed readings of the text I am indebted to Cristina Isolabella,
one of the graduate students in the course on team building, my daughter,
Sharon Hare, and my wife, June Hare, whom I can count on for a careful
reading of whatever I write.

I am indebted to the authors and publishers who made it possible to
include text, figures, and tables from previously published sources. Specific
credits are given in the text.

PART I
GROUPS AND TEAMS

1
Basic Concepts

Social psychologists have been interested in the dynamics of small groups for many years; however, they have only recently turned their attention to teams. One indication of this trend is the year in which each of the terms referring to groups and teams was first introduced in the index of *Psychological Abstracts*. The term "sociometry" first appeared in the index in 1940 with references to the work of Moreno and others; the term "group dynamics" appeared in 1945 with reference to the work of Lewin and his colleagues; and the term "small groups" appeared in 1950 with reference to the work of Bales and others.

The concept of "team" did not appear in the index until 1971, with reference to the "team teaching method" that had become a focus of activity in education. An average of four articles were listed each subsequent year under this heading. However the more general heading of "teams" did not appear in the index until 1988, with reference to twenty-one studies of teams used in clinical practice, sports, business, and military activities. In an article published that same year, Lefton recorded that "the latest 'buzzword' is teamwork" (1988:18) and in a book Reddy and Jamison noted that "team building has come of age" (1988:ix). Their edited volume contains a representative selection of articles on team building.

Sociologists apparently developed an interest in teams at an earlier period since the index to the *Sociological Abstracts* contained listings of articles about teams from 1961 onward and about teamwork from 1962. In subsequent years the abstracts contained an average of five articles per year on teams or teamwork.

Although most of the groups and teams described in the social-psychological literature are relatively "small," with twelve members or less, research on "group dynamics" is not limited to small groups and the term "team" is used in military terminology to refer to "combat teams" of several hundred persons. The focus here will be on "small" groups and "small" teams although there are no theories or concepts that apply only to small groups or small teams, just as there are no special theories of "small" individuals in contrast to "large" individuals. Group size or individual size is one variable among many. Nevertheless, there is some value in focusing on small groups and teams since so many important activities take place in these social configurations. Even though the theories may be general, it is desirable to be able to recognize the manifestations of the theories as they appear in small groups and teams so that one can apply the insights of research and experience.

But what are the differences between groups and teams? All teams are groups, but not all groups are teams. Shaplin (1964:61) in a chapter on team teaching notes a distinction made by Klaus and Glaser that can be used for a start. Teams are formally organized and highly structured, for example, a surgical team in a hospital, a football team, or a police SWAT team. Small groups may be informal or formal. Most groups tend to have limited role differentiation and their decision making depends primarily on individual contributions, for example a jury, board of trustees, or personnel evaluation board. If a team does have minimal role differentiation, for example a wrestling or debating team, the team is likely to be in competition with other teams and to represent some larger organization.

Sundstrom and Altman's definition of a *work group* is an example of a typical description of a team (1989:176). They offer as a minimal definition "a set of individuals with formal shared responsibility for one or more outcomes within an organization." For a more demanding definition, they include the following properties:

1. Perception of the group as a work unit by members and nonmembers.
2. Interdependence among members with respect to shared outcomes.
3. Role differentiation among members.
4. Production of a group-level output (not aggregated individual output).
5. Interdependent relations with other groups and/or their representatives within larger systems.

Larson and LaFasto (1989:19) provide a similar definition: "A team has two or more people; it has a specific performance objective or recognizable goal to be attained; and coordination of activity among the members of the team is required for the attainment of the team goal or objective."

More distinctions between groups and teams can be made after first introducing some theoretical perspectives for the analysis of interpersonal behavior. We will want to be clear about the differences between "nominal" groups, a set of individuals with similar characteristics or whose members perform individual tasks in the presence of others, and functional groups. We also will want to record the differences between teams and crews, such as the crew of a sailboat or an airplane, where the activity tends to involve managing some form of transportation.

GROUP AND TEAM BEHAVIOR

In any theoretical or applied text on groups and teams some basic concepts are described. Activity takes place along a time continuum. Something has taken place before that affects the group or team interaction and something will follow as a result. The activity follows some process and takes place within some group or team structure, represented by the set of statuses and roles of members. Some of the activity is devoted to the task, to achieving the group or team goal, and some to the relationships between members, to the maintenance of the group or team structure.

The development of a theory in social psychology tends to begin with a fairly narrow focus, for example with an interest in the phenomenon of a "risky shift" in group decisions. As more variables are added the theory becomes broader in scope. Different system levels are found necessary to explain behavior: individual biology, personality, group, organization, social system, culture, and environment (cf. Hare, 1976:325-329). The theory spreads over the social-psychological space and tends to merge with other theories that had different starting points. For the present view, we will start with several theories that have their primary focus on different aspects of group and team behavior and show how they tend to merge to account for much of the variance in interpersonal behavior.

The relationships between the different theories and aspects of group and team behavior are indicated in Figure 1.1. The box in the center is the group activity, divided into task behavior, on the top, and social-emotional behavior, on the bottom. The arrow on the left represents the things that have happened before, the inputs. The arrow on the right represents the things that follow, the outputs. In much research the actual group activity is a "black box." Only the inputs and outputs are measured. Within the task and social-emotional areas one can distinguish process (here represented by a wavy line) and structure (here represented by a cube). All small group behavior takes place within the context of one or more larger systems. At a minimum one may need to include an analysis of the impact of the organization of which the group is a part (cf. Sundstrom, DeMeuse & Futrell, 1990:124-126). Environmental factors also may play a part. These larger system levels are indicated in Figure 1.1 by the larger rectangle that bounds the box representing the group.

The theory that is useful in identifying types of task activity is functional theory. The theory that is helpful as a starting point for the analysis of social-emotional behavior is dramaturgical analysis. Exchange theory can be used to describe the main elements in process, both task and social-

Figure 1.1
**Relationships between Different Theories and Aspects of Group
and Team Behavior**

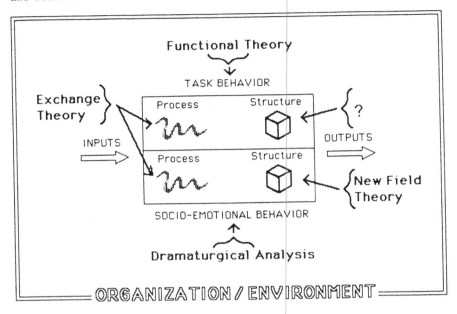

emotional. New Field Theory (SYMLOG) begins with an analysis of the social-emotional structure of groups. At present there is no single theory that has the task structure as its major emphasis, although such a theory should at least recognize contributions to the task at different levels of creativity. A brief introduction to each of these perspectives follows.

THEORETICAL PERSPECTIVES

Functional theory was developed primarily by Parsons to apply to large social systems (Parsons, 1961). However it also can be used for the analysis of behavior in small groups (Hare, 1983a; see Chapter 8). Functional theory describes four basic functions that must be fulfilled for any social system or small group to survive. There must be a set of shared *values* that define the overall meaning and a general pattern to be followed in the group's activity. The group must have sufficient *resources* to meet its goal. The *roles* of the group members must be clear and the members must have a sufficient level of *morale* to work together. Finally, there must be adequate coordination in the form of *leadership* for the use of the resources by the persons playing the roles, guided by the values, to attain specific group goals.

When the fulfillment of each of the four functions is considered as a separate task, then the typical group tends to develop through four phases:

1. Commitment to basic values and overall purpose of the group.
2. Acquisition or development of resources.
3. Defining roles and developing a sufficient level of morale.
4. Carrying out specific group activities, coordinated by leadership.

Eventually groups pass through a final termination phase that is similar to the initial phase. Once more the overall meaning of the group activity is assessed as the group members prepare to go their separate ways.

Each of these phases can be further divided into four subphases with similar functions. For example, to develop a resource, such as a new machine, there must first be a plan. Next tools and raw materials will need to be acquired. Then persons will need to be trained to work together with the tools. In the fourth subphase the new machine is constructed under the leadership of a supervisor.

As part of functional theory, Parsons suggests that the four functional areas be ordered in a cybernetic hierarchy. The function providing the most information is at the top and the function providing the most energy is at the bottom. In this case, the values determine more of the variance in the group's activity than the roles and level of morale. Roles and morale are, in turn, more important than coordination through leadership. The least important are the resources.

Dramaturgical theory reflects the contributions of many persons from social psychology, anthropology, and the theater (Hare & Blumberg, 1988; see Chapter 9). One name that often is associated with this perspective is that of Goffman, who contributed many insights into the processes involved in the "presentation of self in everyday life," especially by the use of informal teams (Goffman, 1959). I have found Moreno's ideas in his descriptions of psychodrama especially useful as a basis for this analysis (Moreno, 1953).

Figure 1.2 includes the main concepts used in dramaturgical analysis. In the center of the figure is a rectangle representing the stage or action area. This can be further divided into two parts, backstage and stage. The backstage area is where the actors prepare for their roles and where special effects are produced to influence the audience. This is the area where those who arrange the setting and provide props, costumes, and makeup do their work. The stage is where the action takes place in full view of the audience. In the social-psychological literature the concept of "territory" refers to the stage and backstage areas that the actors may define for themselves or that may be defined for them (Sundstrom & Altman, 1989). The literature on

Figure 1.2
Basic Concepts for Dramaturgical Analysis

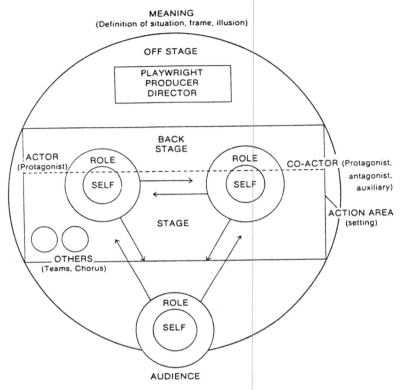

Source: Reprinted by permission of Greenwood Publishing Group, Inc., Westport, CT, from
            Dramaturgical Analysis of Social Interaction by A. Paul Hare and Herbert H.
            Blumberg, p. 7. Copyright © 1988 by A. Paul Hare and Herbert H. Blumberg.

"interpersonal space" is, in effect, a description of the space that an
individual considers optimal for role performance.

For any action there also may be offstage areas where persons who have
organized the activity (producers) and those who have rehearsed the cast
and are providing cues for action (directors) remain hidden from the
audience. In addition, there may be the person who provided the original
idea or script for the performance (playwright). This does not complete the
list, as there also may be persons who cater to the audience.

On stage, in Figure 1.2, there are two sets of nested circles: one set represents the principal actor who is central to the definition of the situation at
the moment (protagonist). The other represents some co-actor, who may be
a protagonist for another idea, an antagonist of the first idea, or an

auxiliary player supporting the protagonist. Inside each of the larger circles representing the roles is a smaller circle to represent the self, the individual characteristics that each person brings to the role. The smaller circles near the protagonist represent additional players who may form a team to support the protagonist or a chorus to echo the mood.

In front of the stage, a set of nested circles represents an audience member. Even if there is no external audience, the actors are themselves an audience for their own and others' actions. Even if no other actor or audience is physically present, all social behavior is performed with some idea of the expectations of one or more reference groups in mind. The large circle, surrounding all the areas, represents the meaning of the event that binds all of the participants together. This overall meaning is variously referred to as the definition of the situation, the frame, or the illusion.

The categories of task activity from a dramaturgical perspective parallel those of functional theory. In the order in which a group would typically deal with them, the tasks are:

1. Developing an *actable idea.*
2. *Staging* by locating or constructing an action area and providing props, costumes, and other necessary equipment.
3. Recruiting *actors*, if they are not already involved in the development of the actable idea, and training them for their *roles.*
4. A period of *enactment* when the "play" is performed under the supervision of the director.
5. A final phase when *new meanings* are assessed for the actors and the audience.

The actable ideas that form the basis of a social drama may be very general or they may be very specific in their implications. At one end of the continuum is an actable idea in the form of an *image* that has a program of action packed into it, much as a symbol in a dream may be a merger of waking events. The idea may be more complex as a *theme*, including a direction of movement and a minimal set of roles to be enacted. The idea may provide the outlines of a *plot*, with a detailed scenario, defined roles, and an indication of the phases the group must go through to reach its goal. At the specific end of the continuum the idea may be as fully developed as a *script* for a play, with parts for each member of the cast and stage directions to guide the performance.

In a group the actable idea may change from moment to moment, especially if the action is guided by an image. Even with scripts, periods of tragedy may be interspersed with periods of comedy or a melodrama may turn to a farce. In addition to their degree of complexity and specificity, the actable ideas also can be identified by the level of creativity required for their enactment. In a similar way each action by an actor can be classified according to the level of creativity required. For dramaturgical analysis five levels of creativity can be identified. Beginning with the lowest level, the categories are: expressive, technical, inventive, innovative, and emergentive. They vary from routine behaviors at the lowest level to providing new definitions of the situation at the highest level. During the course of a group's activity, the behavior of individuals and subgroups can be plotted along a time line using these five levels of creativity (see example in Chapter 9).

In *exchange theory* social interaction is viewed as the exchange of material or nonmaterial goods and services. Major contributors to this theory include Thibaut and Kelley (1959), Blau (1964), Homans (1974), and Emerson (1976). (See Chapter 10.) The category system that will be used here is an extension of the one proposed by Longabaugh (1963). He identified six modalities of exchange: seeking, offering, depriving, accepting, ignoring, and rejecting. In his observations of mother-child interaction he divided the content of the exchanges into four categories: information, control, comfort, and esteem. He later agreed with me that these categories were in effect subsets of the media of exchange associated with functional analysis. At the social system level, Parsons had identified the four media of exchange as money, power, influence, and commitment.

New field theory (SYMLOG) has been developed primarily by Bales (1970, 1988; Bales & Cohen, 1979). (See Chapter 11.) The acronym SYMLOG stands for a SYstem for the Multiple Level Observation of Groups and provides for an analysis of the images that guide interpersonal interaction at the level of the individual, group, situation, and society and in fantasy. It assumes that there are three basic dimensions of interpersonal behavior: Dominance versus submission, positive versus negative, and forward (serious or conforming to the requirements of the task) versus backward (expressive or nonconforming). By dividing each of these dimensions into three segments, high, middle, and low, Bales can identify twenty-six types of individual personalities or group roles. Relationships between individuals or roles or other images can be displayed on a field diagram for the analysis of the extent to which a group is unified or polarized, or contains individuals who are potential scapegoats or mediators. Recent additions to the theory make it possible to identify several hundred types of individuals and provide, through a computer program, a description of how they would be expected to interact with each other.

Prior to SYMLOG most descriptions of the basic dimensions of interpersonal behavior, both verbal and nonverbal, of attitudes, and of values, had identified four basic dimensions (Peabody & Goldberg, 1989). These dimensions were dominance versus submission, positive versus negative, serious versus expressive, and conforming versus nonconforming or some combination or rotation of the four. For SYMLOG Bales used the first two dimensions (dominance vs. submission and positive vs. negative) and combined the last two as forward (serious or conforming) and backward (expressive or nonconforming).

Following Stogdill (1974) almost all other leadership theories concentrate on two dimensions. In SYMLOG terms these are: forward (concern for performance) and positive (concern for people). In these theories the dimensions are measured from zero to forward and zero to positive. There is no description or measurement of either backward or negative behavior. Blake and Mouton's management (leadership) grid is an example (Blake, Mouton & McCanse, 1989). They describe six styles of team leadership behavior based on combinations of these two factors (see Figure 1.3).

Figure 1.3
The Leadership Grid®

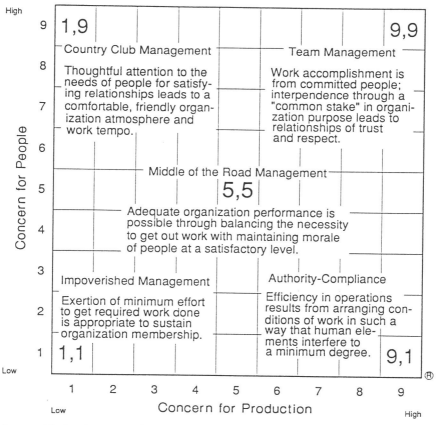

Source: The Leadership Grid® Figure from *Leadership Dilemmas, Grid Solutions*, by Robert R. Blake and Anne Adams McCanse. Houston: Gulf Publishing Company, p. 29. Copyright © 1991, by Scientific Methods, Inc. Reproduced by permission of the owners.

Four of the styles are represented by the corners of the square grid as combinations of high or low concern for people and performance (1,9; 9,1; 1,1, 9,9). A fifth style is represented by a point in the middle of the grid (5,5) where the concerns are balanced. The sixth style is paternalism, a combination of the 1,9 and 9,1 styles.

Elements from functional, dramaturgical, and exchange theories can be combined with the dimensions of new field theory to provide a comprehensive category system for the analysis of social interaction (Hare, 1986a). (See Chapter 12.) The system assumes that individuals can make positive and negative contributions to the task at five levels of creativity and can attempt to persuade others to conform to their ideas using positive or negative reinforcements, also at five levels. All of this can be seen in the context of social exchange.

OVERVIEW OF THE BOOK

Chapter 2 provides a short list of some of the definitions of groups in the social-psychological literature and compares them with definitions of teams in the team building literature. We find that generally no clear distinction is made between the two types of collectives, however the groups called teams appear to have a clearer function, with more role differentiation and more coordination required for their activities. Functional theory is employed to suggest distinctions between various types of teams and crews.

Chapter 3 reviews some of the theories of group and team development. Although five phases in development can be identified, groups may recycle through a phase several times before they are able to move on to the next phase. This process is illustrated with an example of the negotiations at Camp David in 1978, analyzed in terms of dramaturgical analysis.

Chapter 4 compares the method of problem solving in groups, which usually follows the steps in the scientific method, with the process of reaching consensus once individual decisions have been reached, especially for issues that require the commitment of group members. A review of the social-psychological literature on group problem solving is followed by a description of the process of reaching consensus, with emphasis on the way it has been used in the team-building literature.

Chapter 5 is concerned with managing conflict. After introducing some of the approaches suggested by the team-building literature, a brief account of the literature on "pre-negotiation" is introduced to indicate the similarity in the processes of conflict resolution in small groups and in international affairs. The methods of conflict resolution suggested in both types of literature are essentially those of creative problem solving combined with a process of reaching consensus. As an example of the process, a flow chart is described in some detail.

Chapter 6 reviews the team-building literature on consultation. The steps in the process include diagnosis of the problem or problems by collecting data, planning an intervention for a team or organization, and evaluating the results.

Chapter 7 is a case study taken from the files of the SYMLOG Consulting Group as an example of consultation. This chapter completes Part I of the volume, where the primary focus is on teams and team building.

Part II, on theories and applications, is composed primarily of previously published examples of the theoretical perspectives introduced briefly in Chapter 1. The case examples, where they are included, describe collective behavior in conflict situations as well as activity in small groups. Chapter 8 summarizes a functional interpretation of interaction. Chapter 9 introduces a dramaturgical perspective with examples from intergroup relations in Israel. Chapter 10, on exchange theory, includes an example of the analysis of a therapy group. Chapter 11 outlines the main points in the new field theory (SYMLOG). Chapter 12 illustrates the combination of elements of functional, dramaturgical, exchange, and SYMLOG perspectives in one category system with examples from negotiations between Egypt and Israel.

2
Characteristics of Groups and Teams

We discover by reading a variety of texts on group dynamics and team building that few of the authors have attempted to differentiate between groups, teams, crews, and other forms of collective-task-oriented behavior. However the texts on team building usually list the characteristics of effective teams and suggest some of the goals of team building. After considering in turn some of these definitions, characteristics, and goals, an overall scheme, based primarily on functional theory, will be proposed as a way to sort out the differences between groups, teams, and crews.

DEFINITION OF GROUPS

Bales (1950:33) described a group that is small enough for direct observation as

any number of persons engaged in interaction with each other in a single face-to-face meeting or series of meetings, in which each member receives some impression or perception of each other member distinct enough so that he (or she) can, either at the time or in later questioning, give some reaction to each of the others as an individual person, even though it be only to recall that the other person was present.

Cartwright and Zander (1968:48) list a number of characteristics of individuals in interaction. The larger the number of attributes and the greater their strength, the closer the set of individuals comes to being a "full-fledged" group:

1. They engage in frequent interaction.
2. They define themselves as members of a group.
3. They are defined by others as belonging to the group.

4. They share norms concerning matters of common interest.
5. They participate in a system of interlocking roles.
6. They identify with one another as a result of having set up the same model-object or ideals in their superego.
7. They find the group rewarding.
8. They pursue promotively interdependent goals.
9. They have a collective perception of their identity.
10. They tend to act in a unitary manner toward the environment.

After reviewing eighty different definitions of a group, Shaw (1981:8) concludes: "A group is defined as two or more persons who are interacting with one another in such a manner that each person influences and is influenced by each other person."

Hare (1982:20) describes a fully functioning small group in terms of functional theory (AGIL) as one whose members are committed to a set of values that define the overall pattern of activity, have accumulated or generated the resources necessary for the task at hand, have worked out an appropriate form of role differentiation and developed a sufficient level of morale for the task, and have sufficient control in the form of leadership to coordinate the use of resources by the members playing their roles in the interest of the group's values.

DEFINITIONS OF TEAMS

In the literature on teams Dyer (1987:24-25) defines a team as "a collection of people who must collaborate, *to some degree*, to achieve common goals." He goes on to suggest that various types of teams can be placed along a continuum according to the amount of collaboration (integration and role differentiation) required. At one end of the continuum are teams, such as golf teams, that are composed of a set of individual performers. At the other end he places the crew of an Air Force bomber where every member of the crew has a specific set of assignments that are critical if the venture is to be successful.

Bruce (1980:157) in his descriptions of primary health care teams in Britain identified three modes of cooperation: nominal (administrative), convenient (some links between agencies), and committed cooperation. In another area, in his discussion of teamwork at General Foods, Bassin (1988:66) distinguished between several options for business teams:

1. Informal teams—where the product manager is an informal leader for activities such as brainstorming or problem solving.
2. Communication teams—with the product manager as the formal leader.
3. Formalized business brand teams—with the product manager as the formal leader and clear team objectives.

4. Development/venture teams—teams that are regarded as autonomous, fairly independent units that work together over a three- to five-year period.

For some authors the definition of a team is evident in their description of an "effective team." Patten, who wrote one of the early texts on team building within organizations (1981) suggested four preconditions before a group of managers could develop into an effective team.

1. The group must have a natural reason for working together.
2. The members of the group must be mutually dependent upon each other's experience, abilities, and commitment in order to fulfill mutual objectives.
3. Group members must be committed to the idea that working together as a group leads to more effective decisions.
4. The group must be accountable as a functioning unit within a larger organization. (1988a:15)

Patten goes on to state that

the key to the concept of team is communication within the group. There has to be a singleness of mission and a willingness to cooperate. . . . Whereas managers and their subordinates might be able to improve their overall relationships, coordination, and communication in many situations, the word *team* should be reserved for a special type of work group. (1988a:15)

Francis and Young (1979:6-7) reach a similar conclusion. They asked several hundred managers to define an effective team from their own experience. The managers responded that effective teams produce outstanding results and that team members feel responsible for the output of their teams. Francis and Young conclude that a team is more than a collection of individuals. It is an emotional entity. "Occasionally," they suggest, "we meet an exceptional group that combines high morale, effective task performance, and clear relevance to the organization and we award the accolade of a 'team'."

Bassin (1988:65-88) lists five requirements for high performance teams:

1. Vision—the purpose for existence is shared by all members and is more important than or compatible with individual agendas.
2. Perceived dependent need—the problem must require combined talents.
3. Leadership—must embody and model the vision in behavior in the group and transfer responsibility for team development to the team members.
4. Coordination—effectively using and integrating members' resources, planning with clearly defined outcomes, with time set aside to plan ahead.
5. Adjust and adapt—use feedback.

Similar lists of criteria of effective teams are given in many books and articles on team building (see Buhler & McCann, 1989; Chubin, Porter, Rossini & Connolly, 1986; Johnson, 1986; Kazemek & Albert, 1988; Larson & LaFasto, 1989:26; Sedel, 1989; Weisbord, 1985).

CLASSIFYING GROUPS, TEAMS, AND CREWS

As we see in the various definitions of groups and teams quoted above, groups are no different from teams in their basic components. Indeed, in many cases the term "team" is used as a synonym for "group" or "committee" (Kanter, 1983; Zager & Rosow, 1982). However, as we have noted earlier while all teams are groups, not all groups might be designated as teams. The term "teams" seems to be reserved for work groups that are highly visible and require more differentiated roles and more integration of members' activity. Also, sports teams often are cited as models of teamwork.

Since no clear distinctions between groups, teams, and crews are evident in the social-psychological literature, it is possible that dictionary definitions reflecting common uses of the terms may point toward possible distinctions. For example, *The Oxford English Dictionary* (1989), compiled by Simpson and Weiner, records the following uses of the terms:

Group (in general): A number of persons or things regarded as forming a unit on account of any kind of mutual or common relation, or classified together on account of a common degree of similarity (Vol. VI, p. 887). In social sciences: A group of people, esp. a social group or community (Vol. VI, p. 888).

Team: A number of persons associated with some joint action; now esp. a definite number of persons forming a side in a match, in any team sport; hence a group collaborating in their professional work or in some enterprise or assignment (Vol. XVII, p. 692).

Crew (specific or technical uses): a. A body or squad of workmen engaged upon a particular piece of work, or under one foreman or overseer; a gang. b. A team of people concerned with the technical aspects of film-making, recording, etc., for a particular production; freq. with narrower description of function, as camera crew. c. Nautical. The whole of the men belonging to and manning a ship, boat, or other vessel afloat. d. Aeronautical. In full: air crew. The persons manning an aircraft or space craft. (Vol. IV, p. 15)

As with social-psychological usage, in the dictionary sense, the term "group" is the most general and often is used to refer to a set of individuals who have some common charactristic without actually meeting each other. This is the sense in which the term "nominal group" is used in social psychology. The term "team" is more special since joint action is implied, with sports teams being a very visible example. The term "crew" typically refers to a group of persons managing some form of technology, especially forms of transportation such as boats, aircraft, or spacecraft.

Using the functional (AGIL) cybernetic hierarchy, it is possible to make some distinctions (see Chapter 8 for more complete definitions of the AGIL categories). Crews of boats, planes, or spaceships can be placed at the bottom of the cybernetic hierarchy (A level) since their function is bound to a particular type of equipment or technology. (See Figure 2.1.) Change the technology and you change the nature of the team. For example, in the case of an aircrew, a large amount of information about the conditions of the plane and the weather must be processed in a short period of time (Foushee, 1984).

Moving up, at the G level, are work teams in business, manufacturing, health, and education. These teams are bound to a product, an object or the care or education of a person. Change the nature of the product or the service provided and the team must be reorganized. At the I level are sports teams that are rule driven. They produce nothing. But the playing field is usually swarming with referees to ensure that the game stays within the rules. Change the rules and you have a new game (Kew, 1987).

At the top of the hierarchy, the L level, are scientific research and development teams. They are not bound by any existing equipment, products, or rules. Their task is to develop new concepts and discover new relationships between old or new concepts. Wolpert and Richards (1988:9) writing about "a passion for science" suggest that: "Perhaps it is, above all, the thrill of ideas that binds scientists together, it is the passion that drives them and enables them to survive."

In addition to being sorted by functional specialty in the cybernetic hierarchy, crews and teams[1] also can be classified according to the amount

Figure 2.1
Teams Classified according to the Functional (AGIL) Cybernetic Hierarchy

LEVEL	CHARACTERISTIC	TEAM TYPE
L	New discovery driven	Scientific research and development teams
I	Rule driven	Sports teams
G	Product driven	Business, manufacturing, health, and education teams
A	Equipment or technology driven	Crews of boats, planes, or spaceships

of integration and role differentiation required. Although Dyer (1987) merged the two continua, they can be kept separate to form at least a two-by-two table of types of teams that are either high or low on each continuum. Olmsted made this type of distinction for types of group leadership in an early, 1959, analysis of group activity (Olmsted, 1959; see also Olmsted & Hare, 1978:141). More recently Sundstrom and Altman (1989:185) have used this double dichotomy in their typology of work teams.

Sports teams provide the simplest example of this type of classification. (See Figure 2.2.) Golf teams are low on both integration and role differentiation. Synchronized swimming teams are high on integration but low on differentiation. Track teams are low on integration but high on differentiation. Football teams (American style) are high on both the need for integration and differentiation. Each type of team requires a different leader style. For some teams the main function of the members is to support the activity of a central person, such as the surgeon in a surgical team or the pilot of an airplane.

Some systems of classifying tasks combine tasks requiring different levels of creativity in the same category. Once this has been done, it is difficult to sort out the effects of level of creativity on performance (see Chapter 5 for definitions of five levels of creativity). For example, McGrath classifies tasks in four general types (McGrath, 1984; McGrath & Kravitz, 1982): I. to generate, II. to choose, III. to resolve, and IV. to execute. Each type includes several subtypes. Type I, to generate, includes "plans." Plans probably require creativity at the lower levels of 2 (technical) and 3 (inventive). Type I also includes "creative ideas." These would seem to require creativity at higher levels of 4 (innovative) and 5 (emergentive). In contrast

Figure 2.2
Sports Teams Classified according to Required Integration and Role Differentiation

		Integration	
		LOW	HIGH
Role Differentiation	LOW	Golf	Synchronized swimming
	HIGH	Track	Football

McGrath's Type III, to resolve, includes negotiation, bargaining, dilemmas, coalition formation, and allocation. All of these tasks usually are solved by some "trade off," or creativity at level 3. Type IV, to execute, includes contests, competitive sports, wars, and physical tasks. These tasks require creativity at level 2, skill. Overall, McGrath's types seem to be listed according to the average level of creativity involved, with Type I requiring the highest levels of creativity and Type IV requiring the lowest levels of creativity.

NOTE

1. For persons specializing in one of the areas of application for teams, some of the following accounts may suggest advantages and problems:

Business: growing firms (Owens, 1989), hotels (Berger & Vanger, 1986), sales (Greenberg & Greenberg, 1988; Likert, 1967), electric utilities (Miller & Phillips, 1986), credit unions (Gray, 1986), work units in Japan (Kosower, 1987), computer software and data processing (Jacobs & Everett, 1988; Mathews & Vogt, 1987), self-regulating work groups (Pearce & Ravlin, 1987).

Health and social work: child development (Allen, Holm & Schiefelbusch, 1978), disciplinary teams (Horwitz, 1970), preventive care (Bruce, 1980), health service McGowan & Norton, 1989), mental health (Hall, 1985), British area social work (Payne, 1979).

Education: exceptional children (Golin & Ducanis, 1981), college (LaFauci & Richter, 1970), elementary and high schools (Shaplin & Olds, 1964), British secondary schools (Worrall, Mitson, Dorrance, Williams & Frame, 1970).

Research and development: interdisciplinary (Chubin et al., 1986).

3
Group and Team Development

Groups and teams go through a set of phases as their activity develops (progresses) during the course of a single meeting and over the life of the group or team. It is easy to imagine that some types of activity, such as defining the problem, may need to take place at the beginning of a session and that other types of activity, such as preparing to disband, may take place at the end. However, whether or not there has been a typical set of phases that groups and teams go through and how many there are is still a matter of debate. Whatever the typical sequence is, it is clear from the analysis of actual groups that some groups fail to progress beyond the early phases and others may recycle through some of the phases several times before reaching their goal (cf. Hare, 1985b:132-135).

Some of the theories of group development differentiate development with regard to task performance from that focusing on the development of social-emotional relations. In the present text the functional (AGIL) categories are used primariy for the analysis of task behavior and the dramaturgical categories for social-emotional behavior. However, for the first overview of theories, some of the major descriptions of phases are listed as they appear to fit with a five-phase theory.

FIVE PHASES OF DEVELOPMENT

In functional terms the five phases are L-A-I-G with a terminal phase of L (Hare, 1982:76-83). That is, the first phase involves the development of an overall definition of the situation (L-values), in the second phase resources (A) are acquired, then roles and morale (I) are supplied, and then the roles and resources are coordinated through leadership (G). The final L phase deals with matters of termination—at the end of a meeting, if we are analyzing a meeting, or at the end of the group's life if we are taking a longer view. If one wishes more detail, phases within phases can be identified (see Chapter 8).

The dramaturgical phases suggested by Hare (Hare, Blumberg, et al., 1988:3-4) are the same as the L-A-I-G-L sequence but with emphasis on the activity required to produce a social drama. The sequence is: developing an actable idea (L), staging (A), finding actors and assigning roles (I), enacting (G), and evaluating new meanings for actors and audience (L) (see Chapter 9).

An early theory of development based on the analysis of sensitivity training groups by Bennis and Shepard (1956) incorporated their own observations and insights of Freud, Schutz, and Bion. They described two major phases. In phase one the group is dealing with problems of dependence and power relations and in phase two with interdependence and personal relations. Each phase is further divided into three subphases. These six categories do not fit neatly into the five-phase L-A-I-G-L scheme although they do cover the same range of activities from beginning to end.

Tuckman (1965) based his analysis primarily on therapy groups. Initially he identified four phases, each divided by task activity and group structure (social-emotional activity). This theory became popular with team building practitioners and is generally cited by the terms Tuckman used to identify the major themes in the development of group structure: forming, storming, norming, and performing. Later he added a fifth phase of termination (Tuckman & Jensen, 1977).

For team building, Francis and Young (1979:9-11) based their theory of development on that of Tuckman. They identified four phases as: testing, infighting, getting organized, and mature closeness, without a termination phase. Adair-Heeley and Garwood (1989), Drexler, Sibbet, and Forrester (1988), Koehler (1989), and Moosbruker (1988) describe similar four-phase sequences.

Patten (1981:33), in his team-building activity, favored Schutz's (1958) three-phase theory where the recurring problems are identified as boundary problems (inclusion, in Schutz's terms), decision making and power (Schutz's control), and individual or team integration (Schutz's affection). Schutz did not identify a fourth phase of work on the task, but he did suggest that at the end of a group's life, it would progress through the three phases in reverse order: affection, control, and inclusion, as the group members went their separate ways.

Dyer (1987: 67-87) describes the activities in a typical team development program that are, in effect, a general theory of group development. After a period of preparation by the consultant, Dyer identifies five phases: start up; problem solving and process analysis; interpersonal, subunit, and group feedback; action planning; and follow-up.

Gersick (1988), in an analysis of the activities of teams, reports no universal series of phases. She suggests that there are periods of equilibrium punctuated by alternating periods of inertia or revolution. A team's progress appears to be triggered more by awareness of time and deadlines. However, she does note that teams usually begin each phase of work with an agreement on a plan and end with some accomplished product.

Many consultants who do team building seem to favor a theory of group development based on the activities as they would appear in a therapy or sensitivity training group where the leader takes a very passive role and initially the task is not clearly defined for the group members. In addition the members of these types of groups usually come from different organizations and often have not met before. If the consultant is doing team building in a workshop where the participants do come from different organizations and the consultant is using an "experiential" group approach, then these theories may be appropriate at the time. However, they would not provide the best fit with the activity that could be expected when the participant returns to his or her organization and once more takes part in an "intact" team whose members have functionally related skills and specialized roles. For these situations, a more general theory should be more appropriate.

Whatever the nature of the group as defined by its level of activity in a functional (AGIL) hierarchy or its degree of differentiation and integration, it still will face some problems in common with other groups. The nature of the task, group resources, member skills, and member personalities all will affect the time and energy required for the group or team to pass through each of the phases of development. For example, in some cases the basic problem of the group lies in the way the task was designed in the first place, as reflected in the changes made in the production of cars from assembly lines to separate work groups in the Volvo plant in Sweden (Katz & Kahn, 1978:727-737).

GROUP DEVELOPMENT AT CAMP DAVID

The following account of the negotiations at Camp David in 1978 in terms of a dramaturgical theory of group development provides an example of the application of the theory in an actual case. President Jimmy Carter of the United States, President Anwar Sadat of Egypt, and Prime Minister Menachem Begin of Israel and their staffs had assembled at the U.S. presidential retreat at Camp David to draft two accords, one a framework for peace in the Middle East and the other a framework for the conclusion of a peace treaty between Egypt and Israel. The analysis is based on President Carter's account of the meetings (1982).

The case illustrates the fact that groups and teams may not progress through the developmental phases in the expected order on their first attempt. As noted earlier in this chapter, the phases in a performance of a social drama are:

1. The development of an actable idea, that could be in the form of an image, theme, plot, or script.
2. Selection of a stage or action area.
3. Recruitment of actors and training for roles.
4. The enactment.
5. A new definition of the situation for actors and audience.

In this example the stage had been selected by Carter prior to the agreement of the participants on the exact nature of the actable idea in the hope that his version of the proposed activity at Camp David would prevail. In the selection of the stage Carter had assumed the role of director for the performance. Later, when he revealed that the United States was ready to cover the cost of relocating airports that had been built in the Sinai and to provide other types of support, he was taking the role of producer. On those occasions when he helped work out the details of the agreements he acted as an auxiliary player. Thus, in addition to his principal role as mediator, Carter played several other roles. Although each of these roles might have been played by a different person, the fact that Carter could and did play all of them made it possible for him to make contributions from several different perspectives without the necessity of taking the time to bring other persons up-to-date on the state of play. In any instance of mediation, several different system levels are involved. This becomes very obvious in an instance of international mediation. When information is available from all relevant system levels, the chances of a solution at a higher level of creativity are greater.

The activities at Camp David were not those of a single small group whose members came together for a series of meetings that might easily be classified according to the phases of group development. Rather, the activity was carried out within and among three national delegations and their supporting staffs. However all of the participants were at Camp David to implement the same goal so that it is possible to consider all of those present as constituting a single group with the three delegations and the small groups that were formed in the process as subgroups. The three leaders, Carter, Sadat, and Begin, formed the central subgroup. Although this subgroup was only active during the first few days at Camp David, all of the other subgroups worked to help accomplish the task that only the three leaders could carry out: the signing of the frameworks for peace.

The sessions at Camp David were not the first time that representatives of Egypt, Israel, and the United States had met to work on a draft of acceptable peace treaty agreements and they would not be the last. Negotiations already had been carried out through various forms of summits, shuttle diplomacy, and conferences at the ministerial level for about a year. As a result, all three sides had considerable experience in dealing with the issues and with each other.

The Camp David summit was convened as an "all out" effort of the American president to save the peace process. In his view, the impasse in the negotiations in summer 1978 might have led not only to a serious blow to Sadat's regime but also to a new war in the Middle East.

This summit meeting, and indeed any problem-solving session where the participants are drafting a set of procedures for persons in addition to themselves to follow, is in effect a "play within a play." The participants need to develop two actable ideas. One idea is a procedure for group problem solving that will make it possible for the group to reach a decision. The second actable idea is embodied in the image, theme, plot, or script that results from their deliberations. In Shakespeare's play, Hamlet has a small group of players reveal the fact that the relationship between the king and queen does not represent a positive state of affairs. In contrast, at Camp David, Carter hopes to show by the enactments of several small groups of players that the relationships between Sadat and Begin and their countries need not be as negative as they appear to be, and can be turned to positive account.

NATURAL TIME PERIODS

As a first step toward the analysis of phases in group development during the talks at Camp David, the total period of thirteen days was divided into natural time periods. Like the acts and scenes in a play, the beginnings and endings of these natural time periods are indicated by changes in the actable idea, the setting, or the actors. In this case estimates of the natural time periods were supported by asking some of the former participants in interviews what phases they could identify and what characterized the activity during each of these phases (see Hare, 1985b:119-142). By this method, five natural time periods were identified:

1. Days 1-3 when Carter held joint talks with Sadat and Begin.
2. Days 4-8 when Carter and his team were producing the American draft of the proposals, consulting separately with Sadat and Begin and their advisers.
3. Days 9 and 10 when the drafting group featuring Barak (Israeli) and el-Baz (Egyptian) was working on the details of the Egyptian-Israeli agreement with the Americans shuttling between the parties.
4. Days 10 and 11 when the parties were unable to overcome the Sinai issues culminating in the crisis and Sadat then prepared to leave.
5. Days 12 and 13 when solutions were found for the remaining problems and the Camp David accords were signed at the White House in Washington, D.C.

During the thirteen-day period, Carter introduced festive meals, a Marine Corps drill, a trip to the Gettysburg battleground, and various other diversionary activities designed to reduce tension and allow participants to meet socially. However there is no evidence in this case that any of the periods of recreation should be highlighted by considering it a separate phase. Although some of the delegates had especially friendly relationships both within and between delegations, most of these, such as Carter-Sadat and Weizman-Sadat, appear to have been made during the negotiations prior to Camp David. Throughout the summit meeting, the small space, informal setting, and informal code of behavior did facilitate the interaction between delegates.

Part of Period 1 and all of Periods 2 and 3 are similar in that they are each concerned with attempts to produce actable drafts of the accords. They can be seen as a set because they are similar in the controlling idea, but have a different group of actors involved in the task and work at a different level of detail. Although not singled out by the participants who were interviewed, the Carter-Begin meeting of the first evening and the Carter-Sadat meeting of Day 2 both were concerned with gaining commitment to the overall "actable idea." It was during this time that the three main actors had to agree on their reason for being at Camp David. The culmination of the talks at the White House signing ceremony also should be treated as a separate period as this was not only the goal attainment of the conference, but also was held on a different stage before an audience.

Given the amendments to the natural time periods identified by the participants, the group development at Camp David can be divided into seven acts as follows:

Act 1—Day 1 and the morning of Day 2: The activity primarily was concerned with agreement on the actable idea as Carter discussed the purpose of the Camp David talks with Begin and Sadat separately. In dramaturgical terminology, they were outlining the "plot" by indicating the goal and the general procedure for reaching the goal. The main participants had held different ideas about the purpose of the summit before they arrived at Camp David. Carter established that his definition of the purpose would prevail. In this initial act, and on through the second act, Sadat and Begin were performing as heads of states, primarily in the roles of protagonists for the concerns of their own countries, rather than as negotiators, from whom more spontaneity would have been required,

Act 2—The afternoon of Day 2 and Day 3: Carter, Sadat, and Begin initiated the first of four similar phases as they worked on a draft of the documents. This was the first variation of the enactment of the "play within the play." Given that the eventual goal was to sign the accords, two frameworks had to be constructed, one for peace in the Middle East and the other for the conclusion of a peace between Egypt and Israel. However, in this act, Sadat and Begin, as protagonists with opposing views, were unable to agree on a text. The act ended as Carter blocked the door to his study until they agreed to give him one more day to produce a draft. The threat that Sadat and Begin would leave Camp David posed a major problem for the conference and threw it back to the initial phase since a new commitment to a variation of the actable idea was required.

Act 3—Days 4-8: This was the second of the enactment phases of the play within the play as the American team worked on the draft. The act also ended in a crisis, with a return to the initial phase, as Sadat was "troubled" and Carter thought he was ready to leave. Begin proposed that they end the meetings and suggested a draft statement for the press. Carter again had to motivate Sadat and Begin to stay long enough for one more try.

Act 4—Day 9 through the afternoon of Day 10. This was the third session of enactment with Barak and el-Baz doing much of the work, accompanied by Carter and Vance, the U.S. Secretary of State.

Act 5—Evening of Day 10 and Day 11: Because Sadat insisted that Israeli settlements be removed from the Sinai and Begin wanted to leave them there, Carter concluded that there was a deadlock and prepared to end the conference. This meant that they had failed to reach the final objective and the group moved to the terminal phase of establishing the "new meaning" for their relationships. Carter drafted a proposal for the final statement and press release, to be agreed upon in this final phase. However, Sadat and his team packed their bags to leave, throwing the conference back to the initial phase again. Carter once more had to motivate Sadat and Begin to stay until Sunday for closure.

Act 6—Days 12 and 13: During Act 6, two types of activity were going on at the same time. As the curtain rose, most of the participants were preparing their final statements to describe the failure. But as Carter checked the points on which there was agreement, he did not give up hope and pressed to find a solution to the issues of the Sinai settlements and the control of Jerusalem. This was the fourth enactment period, superimposed on the terminal phase. The breakthrough on the settlement issue, of having Begin refer the issue to the Israeli Knesset (parliament), actually had been mentioned as a possibility on Day 7 by Dayan, Israeli Foreign Minister, and Barak but not used. This constituted a major shift in role for Begin, since he was now relieved of the responsibility for making a major decision at Camp David. It was now only necessary to provide options that could be presented to the Israeli Knesset.

The shift in the definition of the situation, by declaring that the decision could not be reached, seemed to take off the pressure so that the participants could have second thoughts, although Carter was pressing Sadat and Begin very hard to find some agreement on the last few points. Fine changes in wording were necessary before agreement could be reached, for example, on the issue of "self-government" of the Palestinians. As major protagonists throughout the conference, Begin and Sadat, and Carter, to a lesser extent, were very sensitive to any words or actions that would not fit the image they wished to project to their respective countries.

Act 7—Evening of Day 13: The final signing of the accords took place. As noted earlier, in addition to a different type of activity, this act is set apart because it is the only one that took place before an audience. It was both the termination of the previous drama and the beginning of a new one.

Acts 1-6 took place backstage as the actors improvised a script for a new production that would involve not only themselves but actors from many countries. After the White House "opening," the show still had to go on the road to gain the approval of Israel, Egypt, and the United States. There was hope that the "spirit of Camp David" (the "illusion" in a theatrical sense) would carry forward to solve the remaining problems of the occupied territories and Jerusalem.

To conclude, the analysis above was begun to test the hypothesis that the problem solving at Camp David would progress through the phases in a typical dramatic production. However, the actual "road to agreement" turned out not to be a wide, well-marked highway but a narrow, hazardous route with many switchbacks that brought the group time and again to the starting point. Although progress through the five phases eventually was achieved, the pattern of Acts took the following form:

Act 1: Actable idea (Carter had already set the stage).

Act 2: Selection of role players, enactment, return to commitment for actable idea.

Act 3: New role players, enactment, return to commitment.

Act 4: New role players, enactment.

Act 5: Terminal phase, return to commitment.

Act 6: Terminal phase, new role players, enactment.

Act 7: Terminal phase of conference, presentation of actable idea for a new international enactment.

4
Problem Solving and Consensus

The scientific method is the most effective method of problem solving when the problem involves objects, for example, in developing a new product or deciding upon a new method of production. Problem-solving methods outlined in the team-building literature tend to reflect this. When the discussion concerns interpersonal relations or if the decision requires the commitment of a team to perform, then the process of "consensus" is best. Although it usually is recommended, either directly or implicitly, there is some confusion about the process and about the outcome. For both the use of the scientific method and consensus, few of the discussions of the process include a recognition that different levels of creativity may be involved or how to achieve them. This chapter begins with a summary of social-psychological research on group problem solving. This is followed by a discussion of the scientific method and the process of consensus as they appear in the team-building literature.

GROUP PROBLEM SOLVING

From the early 1900s social psychologists have been interested in the effect of the presence of other persons on an individual's behavior in problem solving and in other forms of activity. By the 1920s experiments were performed to observe problem solving in groups (Hare, 1976:384-395). The comparison of the individual problem solver with a group has continued

The first part of this chapter, Group Problem Solving, including the comparison of an individual with a group and a group with a group, is based on the survey of the literature on group problem solving in *Small Group Research: A Handbook* (Hare, Blumberg, Davies & Kent, 1992). It appears in the same form in an article on group problem solving in the *Encyclopedia of Sociology* edited by Edgar F. Borgatta and Marie L. Borgatta (New York: Macmillan, 1991).

through the present day since there are economic and social costs in maintaining a group to solve problems. Thus the question remains, for what types of problems are individuals best able to find a solution and for what types is it best to have a group? In answer to this question, a summary of research comparing individuals and groups will be presented first, followed by a comparison of different types of groups (Hare, 1976:chs. 14, 15; Hare, Blumberg, Davies & Kent, 1992:chs. 8, 11, 12).

Individual versus Group

For many group tasks, an individual is first required to reach an individual decision or perform some individual activity before sharing or combining the individual product with that of other group members to form a group decision or a group product.

Thus the first phase of a group task often is carried out by individuals in a group situation. Any effect of the presence of other persons on an individual's activity becomes important at this time. A person performing an individual task in the presence of others may do less well, as well, or better than when performing alone. Zajonc (1965) hypothesized that when subjects are aroused by the presence of others, well-learned or easy (hence dominant) responses would be enhanced by the presence of others, while performance on novel, poorly learned, or complex tasks would deteriorate, since the dominant response would be to make errors. Arousal may be increased because of a drive based on survival or knowledge that others may reward or punish behavior, or because the others distract the subject's attention and it becomes necessary to deal with both the task and the distraction. The performance of an individual in the presence of others is lower if the others interfere with the activity in some way and higher if the others provide high performance role models.

For research comparing the productivity of an individual with that of a group, the task has to be one that is capable of being performed by an individual. There would be no contest if the task required a set of actions to be performed simultaneously that would be impossible for an individual. Thus we should not be surprised to find that, for these types of problem solving situations, an individual can be just as effective as a group.

When individuals are compared with groups on the same task, groups generally are found to be better than the average individuals, but seldom better than the best (Hill, 1982). The productivity of the group tends to be less than that of the same number of individuals if no division of labor is required, if there are problems of control, or if the group develops a norm against high productivity. In terms of the number of individual hours required for a task, an individual is usually more productive than a group. When groups appear to be better than individuals, part of the group effect is simply having a larger number of persons to remember facts, identify objects, or produce ideas, especially for tasks requiring low levels of creativity. The average of a number of judgments is usually more accurate than that of a single individual. In addition, the result of a group decision by majority opinion may be more accurate than that of the average of the same number of individuals since the majority decision will not include deviant opinions that would be included in the average.

The fact that groups do better than individuals on difficult and complex tasks requiring high levels of creativity may result from having at least one skilled problem solver in the group (Laughlin & Futoran, 1985). This is especially true for puzzles for which the correct answer is obvious once one person discovers it. Thus "truth" wins the decision. Groups may do less well if the type of feedback they are given makes it difficult to locate their errors.

Individuals' productivity in groups may be lower if they engage in "social loafing" and put in less effort than they would doing the same task on their own (Latané, Williams & Harkins, 1979). This is more likely to happen if there is shared responsibility for the outcome, if the individuals believe their efforts are dispensable or cannot be identified, or if their motivation is low. These effects are likelier to result with tasks requiring low levels of creativity.

The group process called "brainstorming" was developed as a method of enhancing creativity in a group by having individuals generate ideas without criticism from other group members. However, as with other tasks, sets of individuals working alone produce more ideas than the same number of persons working in a group (Street, 1974). Part of the problem in groups is a "production block" as group members use valuable time as they take turns talking (Diehl & Stroebe, 1987). For both individuals and groups it is easier to produce ideas if there is no limit on their practical usefulness.

Several systems have been suggested to take advantage of the problem-solving abilities of a number of individuals without having them participate in a group discussion. In these "nominal" groups, individual judgments are combined by some system of averaging (Rohrbaugh, 1981).

Some research continues to explore the possibility that individuals will make more "risky" decisions when they participate in group discussion. However the body of research indicates that the factors that influence "choice" in a group are the same as those that influence any other type of behavior, namely attributes of the situation, the group, and the individual (Isenberg, 1986). Individual choices shift as a result of group discussion; they are influenced by social comparison and persuasive argumentation. The process of social comparison appears to involve an exaggerated perception of the group norm on the part of individual members or a shift to a position more extreme than the group norms (over conformity). Group members also are found to be sensitive to the number of arguments in a particular direction as well as to the novelty and persuasiveness of the arguments. Some norms and argument may be sex- or personality-linked and thus only have an effect in particular contexts or with particular tasks.

Group versus Group

Productive groups have a commitment to a clear goal and a combination of members' personalities and skills, type of group structure, role assignment, morale, and problem-solving experience that are appropriate for the task (McGrath, 1984). Although competition between members may result in higher total output, there is usually a cost in terms of low member satisfaction. However if the group members are interdependent and some cooperation is necessary, then competition will lower efficiency (Rosenbaum, Moore, Cotton, Cook, Hieser, Shovar & Gray, 1980).

Groups composed of individuals whose personality traits enable them to take initiative, act independently, and act compatibly with other members will be more productive. When possible, group members will develop a group structure that is compatible with their personalities. For example, members who value authority will create a bureaucratic structure and those who value intimate relations will create a collaborative structure (Friedlander & Green, 1977). When a structure is imposed on a group, productivity will be higher when the structure fits the personality characteristics.

High cohesiveness, measured by members' desire to belong to the group, is associated with high productivity. In sports groups, group success leads to a further increase in cohesiveness.

For a discussion task, a five-member group is optimal (Bales, 1954; Yetton & Bottger, 1983). In general, groups will be less efficient if they have either fewer or more members than those actually required for the task.

Productivity is increased if group members have appropriate information, adequate time for task completion, and a communication network that allows for maximum communication. It usually helps to have a leader designated to coordinate group activity, unless group members are accustomed to sharing the coordination functions. Training for the group task, feedback about the performance, or previous experience with the same task all result in improved performance.

A variety of decision rules have been suggested to increase group efficiency. All have the effect of leading members to a more systematic consideration of the facts and members' abilities. For example, Janis (1982) has labelled as "groupthink" defective policy planning by political decision-making groups. This phenomenon can be avoided if measures are taken to ensure that all negative information is considered thoroughly and group members are given a second chance to express doubts. As a safeguard, more than one set of members and experts may be asked to reach a decision and the results compared.

A decision rule that calls for a majority agreement and one that requires unanimity (all members have, or at least agree to, the same opinion) usually result in the same decision. However, a decision made by consensus (members unite in their support of a decision after a consideration of the needs and interests of the individual members) has been viewed as superior to majority rule in terms of decision quality, valuing of all members, and conflict resolution, although a decision may take longer to reach (Hare, 1982:146-154).

Research on the decisions of juries has been conducted using simulations (Tindale & Davis, 1985). In much of the research no actual interaction between the "jurors" occurs. Typically a court case is compiled with variations in the sex or apparent guilt of the accused. Subjects are then asked to give their verdicts. Aside from the facts that the decision is about another human being, leading to more sympathy for the defendant of one's own sex, and a greater certainty of guilt and willingness to convict if the experimental subject has had actual jury experience, the results of simulated jury deliberations are similar to that of other task groups. It is easier for a jury to reach a decision under a majority decision rule than one requiring a unanimous decision, although under the majority rule there may be a dissatisfied minority. After deliberation, individuals' opinions may become polarized. The initial distribution of opinions among the members of a jury is a good predictor of the final outcome.

As noted in the comparison of individual and group decisions, when the cost of bringing group members together is high, a decision method that combines individual opinions statistically may produce satisfactory solutions. Even without a conscious decision rule, when the answer to a problem is immediately evident, once it has been proposed by one member, the answer will be accepted by the group (the case where "truth wins"). In laboratory groups, when no decision rule is specified, members seem to use an "equiprobability" scheme in which each strategy advocated by a member has an equal probability of being selected (Davis, Hornik & Hornseth, 1970). Group members also try to be fair, allowing most members to reach their own level of aspiration. Resulting decisions are often the median of the individual opinions.

Group success tends to be attributed to the skill and effort of the members. Opposing teams or other external features are likely to be blamed for failure.[1]

SCIENTIFIC METHOD

This section provides a brief indication of the way the scientific method, or some variation of it, has been used by consultants in team building. Dyer's problem-solving method is reflected in his "team-building cycle" (1987:53). The cycle includes identifying a problem, data gathering, data analysis, action planning, implementation, and evaluation. These are the same steps as the scientific method, usually formulated as stating an hypothesis, gathering data, evaluating the hypothesis, and reaching a conclusion. Further on in his text, Dyer (1987:79) is even more explicit about the problem-solving process as he outlines twelve steps for teams to follow. Although the problems identified by a team could relate to the use of technology and resources, the main focus is on intermember relationships (see also Buller, 1986:149).

Francis and Young (1979:88-89) indicate six steps in a problem-solving cycle: objectives, success criteria, information, plans, action, and review to improve. They also provide a questionnaire of ten items to be used in identifying effective problem solving (1979:216-217).

Patten (1981:162-163) states directly that the problem-solving method he recommends is a series of steps that "approximate the scientific method in terms of enquiring about cause and effect relationships that reveal problems." His method includes defining the problem, collecting data, developing alternative solutions, evaluating the solutions, and making a decision.

If the scientific method is to be used creatively by teams, it is best if the team contains creative individuals and the organization makes it easy to be creative by not requiring too much conformity (Steiner, G., 1965). If the organization emphasizes informal coalition formation and peer cooperation, the resulting "teams" can be a device for tapping unexpected individual contributions. Kanter (1983:34) observes that participation in teams, whether formal or informal, "helps ready people for change by giving them a broader outlook and more skills and it ensures that people have information beyond their limited purview." In microcomputer firms the fast decision makers used more information, developed more alternatives, and used a two-tiered advice process (Eisenhardt, 1989). In contrast, in interdisciplinary work groups in a medical setting, physicians made almost all the clinical decisions in an automatic fashion (Fiorelli, 1988).

CONSENSUS

A brief set of suggestions for arriving at group decisions using consensus is given in Figure 4.1 (see Hare, 1982:chs. 9, 10). The process of gathering opinions in a group to reach consensus begins with a recognition of the basic concerns of each individual. Note that in Step 1 (Figure 4.1) the outcome of the consensus process can take two forms. The first choice is a decision that each member of the group can identify with, and thus there is unanimity of opinion. A second choice is a decision that seems to be the best possible at the time, even though some members might wish for a different version of the solution if it were possible. With this form, members are able to unite and will be committed to carry out the decision. The steps in Figure

Figure 4.1
Guidelines for Group Decisions by Consensus in Terms of Functional Analysis

Pattern maintenance (L)

Do: Secure agreement to follow the decision rules for consensus, that is, create a decision that incorporates all points of view or one that all members agree is best for the group at this time.

Avoid: A zero-sum solution or using majority vote, averaging, or trading as conflict reduction devices.

Adaptation (A)

Do: Give your own opinions on the issue. Seek out differences of opinion to obtain more facts, especially from low status members.

Avoid: Arguing for your own opinions.

Integration (I)

Do: Address remarks to the group as a whole. Show concern for each individual opinion.

Avoid: Confrontation and criticism.

Goal attainment (G)

Do: Although the main function of the group *coordinator* is to help the group formulate a consensus on each issue and the main function of the group *recorder* is to record each decision as it is reached, all members should help formulate statements about solutions to which all can agree. Even if there appears to be initial agreement, explore the basis of agreement to make sure there is agreement at a fundamental level.

Avoid: Changing your mind only to reach agreement.

Terminal phase (L)

Do: If consensus is reached, make it clear that each group member is responsible to apply the principle in new situations.

Avoid: Pressing for a solution because the time for the meeting is over. If consensus is not reached, postpone the decision until another meeting and do more homework on the problem.

4.1 follow the phases in the development of an idea according to functional analysis. Step 1 involves commitment to the process (L), Step 2 the gathering of facts (A), Step 3 the relations between members (I), Step 4 reaching a decision (G), and Step 5 the implications of the new decision (terminal L).

The criteria for identifying different levels of creativity in a decision are given in Figure 4.2. The five levels are those identified by Taylor (1975:306-308). His terms are used as labels for each level. For Levels 2 through 5, the first sentence in the definition of the level is also Taylor's. He was concerned with identifying creativity in the larger society. His example for Level 1, expressive, was children's drawings that indicated spontaneity, but where originality and the quality of the product were not important. As an example of Level 2, technical, he cited Stradivari's violin; for Level 3, inventive, Edison's light and Bell's telephone; for Level 4, innovative, Jung and Adler's elaborations of Freud's theories; and for Level 5, emergentive, the work of Einstein, Freud, and Picasso.

In Figure 4.2, the second sentence of each definition indicates the activity that would be associated with the level in a problem-solving group. These definitions are taken from the category system proposed by Stock and Thelen (1958). The third sentence in each definition indicates the activity associated with the process of negotiation and is based on the analysis by Hare and Naveh (1986). It is assumed that negotiations that result in agreements at higher levels of creativity will have a more lasting effect.

A number of techniques have been devised to enhance the creative process. Gordon and Zemke (1986:32-33) describe ten of these: (1) creativity training; (2) brainstorming; (3) morphological analysis; (4) force fit/forced relationships; (5) brainwriting; (6) visualization; (7) lists; (8) lateral thinking; (9) divergent thinking; and (10) synectics (see also Ulschak, Nathanson & Gillan, 1981).

Early in the 1960s, Leavitt, in *Managerial Psychology*, had urged managers in industry to consider the advantages of consensus as a method of reaching group decisions (1972). He noted that most businessmen at that time favored the method of limited discussion and acceptance of majority vote in the parliamentary fashion. When the decision is forced quickly, the minority might psychologically reject the decision and may feel challenged to prove that the majority is wrong. When the time comes for action, they may act in ways to "prove" that the decision cannot be made to work. Leavitt emphasized that "if the group's problems require that every member carry out of the group a desire to act positively on the group's decision, then it is imperative that every one accept, both consciously and unconsciously, the decisions reached by the group" (1972:216). He also noted that if total agreement could not be reached, an acceptable form of consensus is that everyone agree that there is a need for some kind of decision. "Then, at least, the minority has expressed its position, has announced that it is not ready to change that position, has had a chance to express its own feelings

Figure 4.2
Categories for Coding Creativity in Art and Science, Group Discussion, and Negotiation

Levels of creativity (from low to high)

1. Expressive

   Art and science: spontaneous contributions that indicate that a person is warming up for the task.
   Group discussion: work that is personally need-oriented and unrelated to group work or providing background facts.
   Negotiation: suggestions that allow the group to bypass a problem without actually solving it.

2. Technical

   Art and science: contributions or solutions that involve skill and a new level of proficiency.
   Group discussion: work that is maintaining and routine in character. Suggestions for improving interpersonal skills.
   Negotiation: providing a standard "textbook" solution to a problem.

3. Inventive

   Art and science: ingenuity with materials, providing combinations to solve old problems in new ways.
   Group discussion: suggesting alternative ways for solving a problem or clarifying already established plans.
   Negotiation: providing solutions that involve "trade-offs," so that each party receives some gain.

4. Innovative

   Art and science: basic principles are understood so that older theories can be extended to cover new areas.
   Group discussion: active problem solving by introducing unusual points of view.
   Negotiation: "extending the margins" of concepts to fit new situations.

5. Emergentive

   Art and science: contributions that involve the most abstract ideational principles or assumptions underlying a body of art or science.
   Group discussion: work that is highly insightful and integrative. It often interprets what has been going on in the group and brings together in a meaningful way a series of experiences.
   Negotiation: suggestions that allow a group to reach consensus through a new definition of the situation.

about its position, and has agreed that some decision short of unanimity is necessary'' (1972:217).

If a group chooses to make decisions by consensus, rather than by majority vote or by leaving some decisions to subgroups, Dyer (1987:103-104) recognizes two forms of consensus when he suggests that group members should realize that consensus does not necessarily mean that all persons think alike but that after a decision each person can at least agree that ''this is a sound decision—one I am willing to support and implement. It is not exactly what I personally want, but given the range of opinions, the time factor, and the kinds of personalities involved, it is a good, working decision.'' If consensus is not reached, discussion should continue.

Dyer's (1987:75) directions for reaching a team decision on a list of ''agree-disagree statements'' are clearly based on consensus. He suggests that group members read the list of twenty statements, then try to ''agree or disagree *unanimously* with each statement *as a group*. Try especially to discover the reasons for disagreement. Try first to come to an agreement as the statement is written, but if you cannot come to agreement, see if you can change the wording so that all can agree.'' In addition, two of the items on the list reflect the consensus mode. Item 1 states: ''A primary concern of all team members should be to establish an atmosphere where all are free to express their opinions.'' Item 6 states: ''In the long run it is more important to use involvement-participative methods than to achieve specific results by other means.''

Francis and Young (1979:86, 226-227) identify five different types of decision making:

1. Individual decisions: One person, usually the leader, makes decisions and all are expected to follow.
2. Minority decisions: A few persons, possibly a subcommittee, decide for the group.
3. Majority decisions: A vote of more than half of the group determines the decision outcome.
4. Consensus decisions: An entire group considers a problem on a basis of reason and discussion. Each member expresses a view and a decision is made to which all can commit themselves at least in part.
5. Unanimous decision: ''Each person fully agrees on the action to be taken, and everyone can fully subscribe to the decision taken.''

Note that Francis and Young differentiate two types of decisions on which all group members can agree, although they only use the term ''consensus'' for the least satisfactory of the two. I propose using the term ''consensus'' for both types of decision, with the emphasis on the process rather than on the final outcome. In the ideal consensus process each team member not only listens to the concern of every other member, but continually tries to formulate a statement that will incorporate the concerns of all members, perhaps through a new formulation that has not been proposed before.

Patten (1981:129, 133) suggests that for union-management disputes one might ask whether "accommodations to conflict reached through collective bargaining are on the same plane as a consensus developed under conditions of trust, openness, risk-taking, authenticity, receptivity to feedback, and focus on change that are characteristic of OD (Organizational Development)." He also recommends consensus as an alternative to majority rule or sweeping messy issues under the rug.

Whatley and Hoffman (1987:89, 93) report that when Quality Circles were first introduced into a government installation, the union felt threatened since the workers might solve some problems on their own. As a result the steering committee that was formed to introduce Quality Circles included union members.

[They] agreed to operate by consensus rather than majority rule. This assured that any agreements would be supported by all members. Although this method of decision making is usually time-consuming in the discussion phase, it helped insure the smooth implementation of committee decisions. The process was further facilitated by the consultant, who acted as a neutral party.

Since it is important that "consensus" be understood as a process leading up to a decision and not just a final outcome, McGregor's (1960:232-235) description of the characteristics of decision making in effective teams is included here in full:

1. The "atmosphere," which can be sensed in a few minutes of observation, tends to be informal, comfortable, relaxed. There are no obvious tensions. It is a working atmosphere in which people are involved and interested. There are no signs of boredom.

2. There is a lot of discussion in which virtually everyone participates, but it remains pertinent to the task of the group. If the discussion gets off the subject, someone will bring it back in short order.

3. The task or the objective of the group is well understood and accepted by the members. There will have been free discussion of the objective at some point until it was formulated in such a way that the members of the group could commit themselves to it.

4. The members listen to each other! The discussion does not have the quality of jumping from one idea to another unrelated one. Every idea is given a hearing. People do not appear to be afraid of being foolish by putting forth a creative thought even if it seems fairly extreme.

5. There is disagreement. The group is comfortable with this and shows no signs of having to avoid conflict or to keep everything on a plane of sweetness and light.

Disagreements are not suppressed or overridden by premature group action. The reasons are carefully examined, and the group seeks to resolve them rather than to dominate the dissenter.

On the other hand, there is no "tyranny of the minority." Individuals who disagree do not appear to be trying to dominate the group or to express hostility. Their disagreement is an expression of a genuine difference of opinion, and they expect a hearing in order that a solution may be found.

Sometimes there are basic disagreements which cannot be resolved. The group finds it possible to live with them, accepting them but not permitting them to block its efforts. Under some conditions, action will be deferred to permit further study of an issue between the members. On other occasions, where the disagreement cannot be resolved and action is necessary, it will be taken but with open caution and recognition that the action may be subject to later reconsideration.

6. Most decisions are reached by a kind of consensus in which it is clear that everybody is in general agreement and willing to go along. However, there is little tendency for individuals who oppose the action to keep their opinions private and thus let apparent consensus mask real disagreement. Formal voting is at a minimum; the group does not accept a simple majority as a proper basis for action.

7. Criticism is frequent, frank, and relatively comfortable. There is little evidence of personal attack, either openly or in a hidden fashion. The criticism has a constructive flavor in that it is oriented toward removing an obstacle that faces the group and prevents it from getting the job done.

8. People are free in expressing their feelings as well as their ideas both on the problem and on the group's operation. There is little pussyfooting, there are few "hidden agendas." Everybody appears to know quite well how everybody else feels about any matter under discussion.

9. When action is taken, clear assignments are made and accepted.

10. The chairman of the group does not dominate it, nor on the contrary, does the group defer unduly to him. In fact, as one observes the activity, it is clear that the leadership shifts from time to time, depending on the circumstances. Different members, because of their knowledge or experience, are in a position at various times to act as "resources" for the group. The members utilize them in this fashion and they occupy leadership roles while they are thus being used.

There is little evidence of a struggle for power as the group operates. The issue is not who controls but how to get the job done.

11. The group is self-conscious about its own operations. Frequently, it will stop to examine how well it is doing or what may be interfering with its operation. The problem may appear to be a matter of procedure, or it may be an individual whose behavior is interfering with the accomplishment of the group's objectives. Whatever it is, it gets open discussion until a solution is found.

Unfortunately many procedures recommended for decison making, such as the use of "nominal groups" (Ulschak, Nathanson & Gillan, 1981:85-96) only provide for a group agreement on the rank order of given items. There is no possibility to combine items into a new idea, much less look for an overarching solution that combines all points of view in a new perspective. Contributions of individuals who "own" ideas that do not receive a high rank are left out of the process.

The same problem occurs when for tasks, such as the NASA moon walk problem, group members are asked to agree on a rank order of items of equipment needed for survival. There is no provision for the introduction of new ideas and therefore no possibility of reaching "consensus" on a higher level of creativity.

A comparable problem occurs with tasks that purport to demonstrate the advantages of brainstorming. Individuals or groups are given a solution and asked to look for a problem, for example, "What are the uses of a brick?" In actual creative problem solving, the problem first must be identified and then a solution sought (Mumford & Gustafson, 1988:32).

Tasks that are suggested for workshops to demonstrate group decision making are often in the form of "eureka" tasks, where once group members have shared the information on their slips of paper, only one individual is needed to find the solution. Then all will agree (Steiner, I., 1972:23). Practice with more complicated and realistic training tasks would be required for a team with maximum role differentiation and a high degree of integration.

NOTE

1. For additional reviews of the literature on group problem solving see: Brandstatter, Davis, and Stocker-Kreichgauer (1982), Davis and Stasson (1988), Kaplan (1989), McGrath (1984), McGrath and Kravitz (1982), and Silver, Cohen, and Rainwater (1988).

5
Managing Conflict

Methods of managing conflict are the same as those for effective problem solving. If a problem had been solved effectively in the first place, there would be no need for a consultant or other mediator to introduce new methods in the second place. Since most of the conflicts that are of concern to team builders involve interpersonal problems, the ideal conflict resolution method will turn out to be one of using the method of consensus.

First we will note the suggestions made by some of the persons involved in team building for the resolution of conflict and then compare the suggestions with a sample of the literature on negotiation and mediation. The chapter closes with the description of a flow chart for the steps in the creative resolution of conflict.

Dyer (1987:115-118) suggests that a useful way to understand conflict is to view it as a violation of expectations. People have expectations about what is to be done, when it is to be done, and how it is to be done. They may have agreed on the what, but find they disagree on the when or how. Dyer's solution is to turn the disagreement into a problem-solving situation that requires the warring factions to try to work out solutions rather than spend time finding fault, placing blame, or looking for causes. One should avoid ignoring the disagreement, smoothing feelings even though an agreement has not been reached, and forcing an agreement, which may lead to public compliance but private resistance.

Francis and Young observe that a team that practices effective interpersonal problem solving combines both confrontation and care for individual viewpoints. Listening skills are especially important (1979:76). How to confront a team member during a critique is a skill that may need to be learned. Criticism of another person may be withheld because of politeness, fear of "loss of face," a disinclination to "rock the boat," or inadequate skills (1979:96). When the conflict is between groups or teams, Francis and

Young stress the importance of identifying a common objective (1979:115). This is the same process as the one of identifying a common goal within a team that all members can agree with by using consensus.

Among the possible interventions that can be made by a third-party consultant for a team, Patten lists the role of "peacemaker" (1981:102). However, he cautions that the consultant often assumes that "the impediments to consensus and mission-attainment are caused by misunderstandings, unauthentic relations, poor team work, and the like." The consultant, with a background in group dynamics, may be poorly equipped to convert "distributive" bargaining into "integrative" bargaining when objective conditions of scarce resources make win-win solutions very difficult (1981:115). Patten actually says that scarce resources make win-win solutions "impossible." However, the literature on pre-negotiation indicates that there are psychological resources, such as recognition, that can be equally or more important than physical resources. For this reason, I have modified my summary of Patten's statement by substituting "very difficult" for "impossible." During World War II, units of the American Army Engineers often had a sign hanging in their shops that proclaimed: "The difficult we do immediately, the impossible takes a little longer." Whether the conflict lies within a group or between groups, Patten recommends the problem-solving mode "to identify a solution that satisfies shared criteria" rather than using persuasion, bargaining, or politics (1981:116-117).

PRE-NEGOTIATION

Although reaching "win-win" solutions is often the stated goal in advice for mediators and negotiators, some of the advocates of this form of negotiation seem to have despaired of having the parties in conflict use this method once they reach the negotiating table, since each side is usually intent on obtaining the best bargain for its side. Thus they recommend that the basic process leading to a "consensus" decision be introduced during the "pre-negotiation" period (Hare, 1989b). The methods used in negotiation are essentially the same whether the dispute is between individuals (e.g., Merritt, 1987), small groups, organizations (e.g., Blake & Mouton, 1984), communities (e.g., Beer, J., 1986), or nations or larger entities. In the instances cited below, the focus generally has been on negotiations between nation states.

In its broadest sense, "pre-negotiation" includes all the activities that take place before the parties in the dispute can get to the table to negotiate a settlement. Stein summarizes:

The process of getting to the table performs important structuring activity as leaders explore an option of negotiation. It reduced uncertainty, clarifies risks and costs, and structures complexity as leaders contemplate the boundaries of the table, who is likely to be there, the rules, and what is likely to be out on and left off the table. (Stein, J., 1988)

As part of this process, Azar (1985:69) emphasizes the importance of "face-to-face exploration into the needs of the opposing parties and the ways and means of satisfying them." Rothman (1989) suggests that it is useful to define pre-negotiation prescriptively in terms of three separate but interrelated phases: (1) *diagnostic*, during which the parties jointly articulate the underlying concerns and issues and attempt to derive shared definitions of the conflict, (2) *procedural*, when the process and the issues to be addressed at any given phase are decided (some issues may be addressed through cooperative-integrative solutions and others through competitive-distributive solutions), and (3) *agenda setting*, when representatives of both sides work separately and with their counterparts to determine priorities and plan the details of the forthcoming negotiations.

Montville (1987:7-8) refers to pre-negotiation as "track two diplomacy," the "unofficial, informal interaction between members of adversary groups or nations which aim to develop strategies, influence public opinion, and organize human material resources in ways that might help resolve their conflict." He suggests that there may be several types of processes including problem-solving workshops that bring together members of the groups in conflict, attempts to influence public opinion, and cooperative economic development. McDonald (1989) expands the list by identifying five tracks of diplomacy: (1) between official representatives of nations, (2) unofficial problem-solving workshops, (3) contact and cooperation through business and other economic ventures, (4) people-to-people exchanges, and (5) information in the press and other media that provides new understandings of the sides in conflict.

Thus at the national and international level, a wide range of activities might be carried out under the heading of "pre-negotiation." However, much of the experience to date comes from the use of the *problem-solving workshop* by Burton (1985), Kelman (1987), Fisher (1987), and others. For a workshop, persons associated with all sides of the conflict are brought together for a series of discussion meetings under the guidance of a third party who is often a university professor. The discussions usually are held in a fairly isolated conference center. The participants may be university students, community leaders, or even government officials who are acting in an unofficial capacity. The workshop has two goals, one to introduce a problem-solving mode of discussion rather than competitive bargaining, and the other to "enable the parties to the conflicts to ascertain the hidden data of their motivations and intentions, and to explore means by which human-societal needs held in common could be satisfied" (Burton, 1985:54).

When the persons present at the workshop include some of the same persons who will later be involved in the negotiations, then there is the hope, often realized, that the pre-negotiation experience will lead to more comprehensive and more satisfying solutions to the conflict. However, when the persons at the workshop are quite different, say university students, then there remains the problem of transmitting the insights from this "diagnostic" phase to the "procedural" and "agenda setting" phases.

Fortunately, the management of conflict in groups, teams, and organizations is not as complicated as that with national or international problems since fewer social system levels are involved. However, the experience with negotiation in larger systems is included here to emphasize the point that a problem-solving approach has been found to be the most productive when it can include attention to the basic needs and concerns of each of the parties. This is the focus of the method of consensus.

CREATIVE SOLUTIONS TO CONFLICT

A set of guidelines that I have proposed for creative solutions to conflict were described in some detail in my book *Creativity in Small Groups* (Hare, 1982:174-180). As an integration of the ideas about conflict resolution in groups or between groups and ideas about creativity in the solution of physical or social problems, I provided a flow chart, as one would for a computer program. The flow chart indicates in outline form the steps that may be involved in the creative process, while the text gives some details of the activities for each of the steps. The problem-solving steps would be the same for an individual who is trying to find a creative solution to a physical problem. However, at least with social problems, it is better if the individual involves others in the process at every possible point.

In outline, the major steps in the creative process are:

1. Define the problem.
2. Collect data from relevant sources.
3. Question: Is a solution available in the system?
4. If the answer is no, use a creative problem-solving routine: (a) skill level, (b) combination level, (c) extension of theory, or (d) new theory or system (branch out of the routine when the problem is solved and go on to Step 5).
5. If the answer is yes in Step 3, or if a solution is found in Step 4, try a pilot project.
6. If the pilot project is a success, secure agreement and commitment to the solution.
7. Implement the new system.

The first step in the creative sequence is to define the problem that requires a creative solution. In some cases the problem may be presented by some other individual or group. In others, the realization that there is a problem may result from something that happened to you personally, or the problem may grow out of the practical or theoretical concerns of an individual or group.

The second step is to collect data concerning the problem from relevant sources. Although groups may be able to provide solutions to all sorts of problems, they are probably most effective in the solution of social problems where the characteristics of the observer (such as age, sex, social class, ethnic group) have more to do with the collection of data than in the solution of physical or environmental problems. That is, with a social problem, the members of the group can use the diversity of their own backgrounds to provide leads concerning the importance of different types of data as well as to facilitate communication with persons of diverse backgrounds who may be important sources of information. For example, in some cultures, people under thirty years old find it easier to relate to others who are under thirty, or women prefer to talk to women, or persons of ethnic minorities may feel that they can trust someone only of their own background.

Thus for the second and subsequent steps, it is best to compose a group following Thelen's (1949) "principle of least group size" that is relatively small and yet contains persons who will be able to make contact with all sectors of the group, organization, or larger social system that have an interest in solving the problem or are important for its solution. The team members also should indicate clearly the kind of value framework in which they hope the solution will be found.

In addition to obtaining the basic demographic data about each sector of the social system, the team members also can interview representatives of each sector to record their ideas about the nature of the problem, their own aspirations concerning a solution, their perceptions of the others involved, and their accounts of factors that seem to be blocking movement towards a solution. With this information in hand, each team member can then write a "position paper" outlining the views of each sector in turn. The papers for each sector should be checked with representatives of each sector to ensure their accuracy. If there is a conflict between groups, these statements may be polemic in nature. It is important to write down the opinions at this stage so that each side knows that the third party understands its position.

Once this has been done, the papers can be filed or perhaps circulated without comment to all groups involved. The statements are unlikely to provide a basis for a solution to the problem since they will not yet contain all the facts that will be necessary. It is probable that both sides, especially if they have had legal training, will not have included any information that is totally false, but they probably will have stressed things that are true and will support the position of their side.

In a conflict between large groups or sectors of a society, it is possible for a relatively small group to accumulate more information about a problem than any of the parties involved for several reasons. First, as a third party, the group will have access to information from all sides, whereas each side is usually limited to information about its own affairs. Second, a specialized group may have more time to devote to the problem than members or leaders in an organization or community who have other day-to-day problems to which to attend. Third, the group may include specialists who have not been previously available to work on the problem.

Once the group is clear about all aspects of the problem, it is time to move on to Step 3 to see if a solution is already available in the system or can be borrowed from another system. As Schmuck, Runkel, and Langmeyer (1971:185) have observed, there may already be some person or some group within the system that has a solution to the problem. Because the person with the solution is considered deviant, of low status, or is outside the general communication network, the solution may not have been utilized by the system. In such a case, it is only necessary to facilitate the acceptance of the idea by moving on to Steps 5, 6, and 7.

If no solution can be found inside the system or can be borrowed from another system, then we proceed to Step 4, which is a "package" of problem-solving routines for different levels of creativity (see Chapter 4). The group tries to find a solution at the lowest skill level and if that fails, then moves to higher levels in turn. Whenever the problem is solved, the group branches out of the subroutine package and continues with Steps 5, 6, and 7. That is, if there is no solution at the skill level or if this level is inappropriate, then try the combination level. If a combination of older forms does not work, then try for an extension of existing theory or cultural forms or laws that might apply in the new situation. If that fails, try for a new understanding of the basic principles in the form of a new theory or a new system.

As a central part of the process, some "creative shift" will be necessary at all levels. At the skill level the relationship to an object or a person may remain but the *form* will have changed, and must be seen to have changed, for example, in acquiring new sensitivity to the feelings of others through "sensitivity training." For a new combination, the group can use the old perception of the forms but needs a new perception of the *relationships*. For an extension of theory, the group needs to redefine some action as an instance of the application of a theory or to give a different valuation to existing relationships. Thus some changes in ideas about both *forms* and *relationships* are required. Finally, a new theory requires some *new forms* (units) and *new relationships*, as in Guilford's (1975:39) creativity level of "implications," which involves the redefinition of units.

There are mechanisms that can be used by groups and individuals to stimulate creativity at each of the levels included in Step 4. For an increase in social or technical skills (technical level) that may produce a more effective system, the workshop approach often is used. Persons who are judged to need skill training join with experts for a few hours, or days, or weeks, depending on the nature of the skill, to learn the new skills and to practice them on simulated problems. If increased skill in interpersonal relations is required, the workshop group itself is often the focus of attention.

"Brainstorming," "creative problem solving," "synectics," and similar methods (Stein, M., 1974, 1975) can be used to find creative solutions, primarily for physical problems, when new combinations are required (inventive level) or when theories need to be extended (innovative level). However the main emphasis in these techniques is on finding new combinations of objects by "joining together apparently irrelevant segments" (Gordon, W., 1961). If the problem is social rather than physical, then one is assuming at the third (inventive) level that the persons involved have the necessary social skills, but that some reorganization or extension of these skills is required; or perhaps it is necessary to compose new groups or sets of persons with all the required skills to realize the solution.

When the problem requires creativity at Level 4, the extension of theory (innovative) or Level 5, the development of a new theory or system (emergentive), then the scientific method is best for the solution of physical problems and the method of consensus the most sensitive for social problems. To extend a current theory to provide a solution for a current problem, one searches through available theories in physical or social science or looks for a precedent in religion, law, politics, or economic practice. For this purpose, a panel of experts who are familiar with the various theories that might have some application can be consulted.

For the development of a new theory or a new form of social organization, the steps in the scientific method as it applies to physical or social phenomena are set out in many methodology texts. The four steps in the method, as they have been summarized by Morris Stein (1974) are: (1) preparatory, (2) hypothesis formation, (3) testing, and (4) communication of results. Some guidelines for the use of the consensus method have been presented earlier in Chapter 4. The goal of the consensus method is to design a "non-zero-sum" game in which all players can see some benefit. This new system or form of relationship is not necessarily what can be true today, but what might be true if people behaved differently. Finding a solution by consensus may take some time. However, developing a new theory in physical science also can take some time.

To facilitate the "creative shift" at all levels of creativity and especially the fifth, it is well to allow time for individual withdrawal between periods of intensive group activity (or work on the problem if only one individual is involved). The individual withdrawal could be to connect with the "outside" through solitary contemplation of the natural surroundings, or to connect with the "inside" through methods of inducing "dreamlike" states without the debilitating effects of drugs. One's natural dream states at night also should be analyzed for potential solutions.

If the problem-solving routines in Step 4 yield more than one solution, you may wish to try out more than one pilot project and then include the ultimate decision about the "elegant" solution as part of the process of securing agreement and commitment from the people involved in Step 6. If enough individuals or groups are available for the creative effort, you may wish to have someone search for a solution on the basis of some cost-benefit analysis. In any event, once a solution is in hand, one is ready to proceed with the final three steps of the pilot project, securing agreement and commitment and implementing the new system. Each of these steps will be facilitated if key people from the community have been involved in the project from the beginning.

6
Consultation:
Diagnosis and Planning

TYPE OF CONSULTATION

As an indication of the complex nature of the consultation process, Blake and Mouton (1976:4-7) present a "consulcube" in which they identify 100 different types of consultation. One dimension of the cube consists of types of interventions:

1. Acceptant—give client a sense of personal security.
2. Catalytic—help collect data to reinterpret assumptions.
3. Confrontation—challenge value-laden assumptions.
4. Prescription—tell client what to do.
5. Theories and principles—as a basis for diagnosis and planning.

A second dimension of the cube lists focal issues:

1. power/authority
2. morale/cohesion
3. standards/norms
4. goals/objectives

The third dimension of the cube is a list of the units of change, that is, the system level that is the focus of the intervention:

1. individual
2. group or team
3. intergroup
4. organization
5. larger social system

In their text on methods of consultation, Blake and Mouton take the reader through each of the 100 cells in the cube with examples of the types of problems that may be faced and suggestions for dealing with the problems.

Whatever the type of intervention, the basic steps in the consultation process, as outlined by Phillips and Elledge (1989),[1] are:

1. Getting started.
1. Data collection.
3. Analyzing the data.
4. Giving feedback.
5. Implementation.
6. Follow-up.

On the side of the boss, Reddy and Burke (1988) recommend that the boss conduct an intensive interview with the prospective consultant before engaging one to determine the consultant's personal background and training experience and the methods the consultant intends to use. Byrd (1988) provides a set of tips on how to avoid having the consultant take over the group. Palmer (1988) outlines steps to follow for a manager who wishes to build a team without the aid of a consultant.

Effective consultants combine some basic model of leader or group behavior with practical experience in helping people solve problems in groups and get along with each other. Blake and Mouton provide an excellent example of this with their use of the "management grid" (Blake, Mouton & McCanse, 1989) in a variety of settings including corporations (Blake, Mouton, Barnes & Greiner, 1964; Blake & Mouton, 1968) and universities (Blake, Mouton & Williams, 1981). Blechert, Christiansen, and Kari (1987) use systems theory as a basis for their approach. Of the various theories available for group and team diagnosis, the new field theory of Bales and his associates in the SYMLOG Consulting Group (Bales & Cohen, 1979; Polley, Hare & Stone, 1988; Hare, 1989a) is the only one that makes it possible to consider both leadership and team dynamics at the same time.

METHODS FOR TEAM DIAGNOSIS

The methods for team diagnosis are the same as those for a group or for any form of collective behavior. They include all the methods used by social psychologists to collect data concerning human behavior. However, the methods recommended by team-building consultants often are designed to be used by members of a team without the aid of a consultant or by a consultant with little formal research experience. Thus they are usually fairly simple to administer, require little time, and are easy to summarize. Phillips and Elledge (1989) in *The Team-Building Source Book* provide guidelines for the basic types of data collection, namely interviews and questionnaires. Additional descriptions of methods are given by:

- Dyer (1987:42-46, 54, 78), who suggests the use of a checklist of problems, interviews, case material, and available records of performance.
- Francis and Young (1979:ch. 2), who provide a 108-item team review questionnaire that covers twelve characteristics of teams from leadership through intergroup relations.
- Patten (1981:24-25), who recommends the use of surveys, interviews, questionnaires, and observation.
- Blake, Mouton, and McCanse (1989:78), who list four methods for team diagnosis: interviewing, in situ diagnosis, simulation, and participant observation. In their case, the questions they ask and the behavior they observe help to place a manager's leadership style as one of the types on the "Managerial Grid" (Blake & Mouton, 1985).

The results of team diagnosis may indicate that the major problem is not with the team but with the support given by the organization or even in the extent to which the whole societal culture endorses team activity. Patten (1981) reminds the consultant that the manager of an organization and the organization's culture must be supportive of team building if it is to be effective. If this is not the case, the consultant may need to begin with some change in the total organization such as clustering groups (Lau, 1988a, 1988b), providing group therapy for managers during periods of change (Hallstein, 1989), introducing "transition meetings" when a new boss arrives (Looram, 1985), supplementing a Quality Circles program with team building (Miskin & Gmelch, 1985; Roth, 1989; see also Inglesby, 1989), or team building in voluntary organizations that serve persons at risk (i.e., retired, unemployed, criminals, etc.) (Schindler-Rainman, 1988).

In addition, the task of the set of persons under diagnosis may not require a team effort to complete. Casey (1985) urges managers to consider whether or not it is necessary to have all executives learn team building. Teamwork may be necessary only as a management group faces real problems that require all the expertise available. He notes that the everyday mode of cooperation that most management groups use is political skill, usually in a series of person-to-person negotiations.

FUNCTIONS OF EFFECTIVE TEAMS

Effective teams, like effective groups, are those that best meet their functional requirements. Although these criteria can be summarized in terms of the four AGIL functions, most of the literature on team building contains longer lists with little indication of which of the items may be similar or dependent upon each other and which of the items represent quite different areas. If the lists are coded according to the AGIL categories (see Chapter 8), the category of resources and task-relevant skills (A) is usually under-represented. This probably results from the consultants having back-grounds in social science; they are prepared to deal with the "group dynamic" aspects of team functioning rather than with the task ability of the members.

The list of six areas of organizational difficulties identified by Blake, Mouton, and McCanse (1989:77)[2] can be used as an example of coding according to AGIL categories:

Organizational Difficulty	AGIL Category
1. Power/authority	G
2. Norms/standards	L, I
3. Cohesion/morals	I
4. Differentiation/structure	I
5. Goals/objectives	L, G
6. Feedback/critique	All categories

Dyer (1987:98-100) contrasts eleven reasons why people do not like to serve on a committee or task force with eleven reasons why they might. If these reasons are coded by functional category we see that the effective team has clear overall goals (L), has appropriate materials and member qualifica-tions (A), is relaxed (I), and has appropriate leadership for implementation (G).

In a similar way, Francis and Young (1979:60-61) suggest that a mature and effective team will have "achieved definite progress in the following distinct areas." They list twelve areas that represent aspects of the four functional requirements. Patten (1981:14-15), making an even finer break-down of criteria, compares twenty characteristics of healthy and unhealthy organizations, focusing on the way teams operate within the organizations.

DIAGRAMS AND REPORTS FOR DIAGNOSIS

The consulting groups that provide special questionnaires or observation forms for team diagnosis also provide diagrams and reports based on the data, usually for a fee. University Associates will score their leadership questionnaire (Kouzes & Posner, 1988) and sum the results in a report. Blake and Mouton (1985) summarize their type of analysis in terms of the Management Grid. Teleometrics International uses a triangular diagram, where the three points of the triangle represent participation, commitment, and creativity, to provide a quick assessment of the overall health of an or-ganization and of those dimensions of competence needing immediate attention (see Moskal, 1987). The SYMLOG Consulting Group, through its authorized consultants, produces a variety of team reports from ten to fifty pages in length featuring field diagrams showing the relationship of group members to each other and bar graphs summarizing the behavior or value characteristics of individuals or teams (see Chapters 7 and 11).

PLANNING

Planning for team building uses information from the team diagnosis (Woodcock & Francis, 1980). Before beginning the team building it is well to ensure that the team has been properly composed for the task at hand. Ideally a team leader has been chosen whose style fits the project—or who can be taught (Lee, 1989), the team members have appropriate skills, and the team is not so large that communication or control becomes a problem (Hackman & Oldham, 1980:171; Hennefrund, 1985).

As noted earlier, if the culture of the organization is not ready to receive a team approach, then one may need to start with a plan for a change in the organization or at least initiate simultaneous activity before beginning team building with a particular group of persons. Otherwise the newly developed "team" may find that it cannot function in the current organizational environment. For example, Hagen (1985) indicates that a business that extols individual initiative can make teamwork difficult and group identification can be inhibited by the existing stratification and specialization of employees. Chance (1989) suggests that rather than giving merit pay and bonuses that reward individual performance, there should be incentives based on the performance of the team as a whole. Dannemiller (1988) cautions that in old-line organizations, the consultant may first need to break down highly structured ways.

At the other extreme, an organization or culture may be very supportive of teamwork. Geber (1989) reports that a team-building course that was used in many locations by the Johnson Wax corporation in the United States was not used in Brazil. This was because Brazil's culture is imbued with the idea of teamwork. Asking employees to take a team-building course would be redundant and possibly insulting.

A problem in the early days of the group dynamics movement was that an individual from an organization would receive training at Bethel in Maine during the summer, only to discover on returning to the organization that there was no receptivity to the new point of view. To partially overcome this problem, pairs of individuals were invited to the group dynamics workshops so that at least there would be someone in the organization who shared the "group dynamics" experience.

Program Design

If the team-building program is for a new team, then the workshop will need to start with "square one" by building commitment to the overall goals of the team (cf. Adams, 1988). However, if the program is for an existing team, then the first phases of team development could be reviewed before concentrating on the phase that has been diagnosed as the primary problem.

In either event, it is well to begin with "contracts" with the team members. These are sets of rules that regulate the purpose of the relationship and define acceptable behavior. Oliver and Langford (1987) recommend two contracts. A task contract deals with the goals and the strategy of the team and a personal contract deals with the dynamics within the group. The personal contract can establish "safe areas" where team members feel free to be open and share personal information.

As Dyer and others suggest, it is important to have a key official in the organization announce the team-building program (Dyer, 1987:49; Pati, Salitore & Brady, 1987:84). The wording of this "call" for the activity, however short, will have a major influence on the way the program is received and the way team building actually develops. Dyer, and most experienced consultants, recommend that the first team-building exercise be held "off site" in some location that stresses informality and makes it easier for the team members to put aside their formal roles. Dude ranches are choice meeting sites for reclusive groups who want to get away from it all (Broadwell, 1989).

Although many organizations use simulations, role playing, and a variety of business games during their team-building workshops to sharpen skills and improve the performance of employees, Broadwell (1987) notes that the opponents of business games think that real experiences in the field are more effective than simulations. George (1987) recommends designing team-building experiences without the "tears" of sensitivity training or the "tinkertoys" of simulations. He lists various things that can be done to enhance team building in the course of the team's everyday life. Team members can enjoy their time together at meals and by sharing jokes and cartoons. Identification with the team can be symbolized in logos and mottos and by social symbols such as rituals, ceremonies, and awards. Work spaces of team members can be placed close together so that they share the same "territory." They also can act as a team in intramural sports and games. A similar list of activities is suggested by Belzer (1989). Davidson (1985) recommends team building with a focus on an actual organizational task of a work unit that can generate harmony and cooperation as by-products. Simply inviting people from all organizational sectors to a meeting can support team performance since socialization, an important part of every meeting, can bring team spirit with it (Conlin, 1989).

Tolle (1988; Wolff, 1988) asserts that "there is no support for the belief that interpersonal team building produces lasting benefits for the organization."[3] He therefore urges managers facing difficulties in their research groups to consider as an alternative to team building a four-step process that involves:

1. Defining the mission in the form of a statement that tells what the group does and why it exists.
2. Developing goals as ideal states to be achieved at some unspecified time in the future.
3. Setting objectives as measurable activities required to make progress toward distant goals.
4. Charting responsibilities concerning who is to do what.

However Tolle does advocate carrying out these four steps in a workshop setting to ensure that everyone in the group has an opportunity to discuss the issues (see also Davidson, 1984).

If games and simulations are used, it is better if they duplicate the actual problems faced by the team. Unfortunately many of the games that purport to give a team experience in creative problem solving (such as moon walks and cave rescues), as noted previously, limit the team to low levels of creativity since the task involves ranking fixed lists of items or using a given set of rules with no provision for combining ideas or introducing new ideas or utilizing given resources in a different way.

Some of the team-building exercises are designed to illustrate a particular theoretical idea. Nanda (1986) has designed a task based on the belief that the performance of supervisors and their workers is influenced by perceptions of each other's roles and responsibilities. Mitchell (1986) describes a team-building intervention based on the theory that disclosure of internal frames of reference improves group members' working relationships.

Many of the "exercises" that are recommended for team building are the same as those used in an earlier period for "sensitivity training," since helping team members "keep in touch with thoughts and feelings" is still considered as important as developing group problem-solving skills (Lau, 1988a, 1988b; Orpen, 1986).

Team-building Workshops

A typical team-building workshop takes place at some off-site location for three or four days. The expense of bringing the team together can make a two-day program too costly and after about four days the manager and the team members are eager to go back to work. Some organizations bring along their own set of computers so that executives can keep in touch with their back-home situation through electronic mail as well as by phone. However, too much time out to deal with back-home problems, especially by the head of the organization, can seriously reduce the effectiveness of the exercise.

The team-building sequence used by University Associates (Frame, Hess & Nielsen, 1982:57-64), for example, begins with four activities that occur before the actual team-building workshop. First, a consultant visits the organization that desires team building to develop a contract and discuss needs and expectations (although for organizations that have many team-building activities, this step may be conducted by phone). Second, a "pre-work" session is held with team members to exchange information about the forthcoming team-building sessions and develop a list of ten to twenty questions to be used by the consultant in individual interviews. The questions will cover key areas of goals, priorities, work load, role clarity, decision making, and conflict management. Third, the consultant interviews each member of the work group and compiles responses into a report. Fourth, data feedback is given by distributing copies of the report for all members to review the night before the off-site meeting. A consultant is cautioned not to distribute the material until the group members are ready to leave their offices the day before the meeting. Otherwise they might engage in counterproductive, premature exchanges that the consultant cannot monitor.

The next set of activities takes place at the off-site meeting. The data are analyzed to identify key strengths and problems. An agenda is developed by rank ordering the problems according to importance. Each key problem is then discussed in depth and ideas are generated for solving each of the key problems. These ideas are then translated into a written action plan for each problem that addresses the following questions:

1. What is to be done to solve the problem?
2. How will it be done?
3. Who will be involved and/or responsible?
4. When will it be completed?

To conclude the workshop, the consultant assists the team members in evaluating the process in terms of their original expectations and other criteria such as the effectiveness of the sessions. From three to nine months after the workshop, depending upon the nature of the action plans, a review session is held to evaluate the extent of the follow-through on actions that were planned.

For University Associates, the discussion session on these topics held during the workshop will be interspersed with "experiential" learning sessions emphasizing group dynamics. Other consultants may rely more on management games and simulations to illustrate the principles of good teamwork. If the consulting group used a particular theory and set of instruments for data collection and analysis, the workshop would include sessions during which the team members would become familiar with this perspective. For example, if Blake and his associates were conducting the workshop, team members would be asked to read about the Management Grid before attending the workshop and would use the grid as a framework for various activities during the workshop (Blake, Mouton & McCanse, 1989:116-126). If the SYMLOG Consulting Group were conducting the workshop, time would be spent introducing Bales's field theory (see Chapters 7 and 11). Patten would stress management by objectives (MBO) in his workshops (1988a, 1988b).[4]

SPECIAL PROBLEMS

In addition to the basic concerns of developing group problem-solving skills (Friedlander, 1966), satisfactory interpersonal relations, and methods of managing conflict (cf. Lefton, 1988), the consultant for team building also may have to deal with special problems such as overcoming unhealthy agreement or dealing with very difficult group members. As part of their discussion of ways of dealing with conflict in a group, Blake, Mouton, and McCanse (1989:155) observe that "achieving effective cooperation when problem-solving relations have broken down can be extraordinarily complicated."

Dyer (1987:141-153) devotes a chapter in his book to the problems of overcoming unhealthy agreement. This problem is manifest when a team makes poor decisions, not out of open conflict, but because the team members pretend to agree when they really do not. The symptoms of this state of affairs, such as the feeling of frustration by team members, the reluctance to say what they really mean during team meetings, and the tendency to blame others outside their group for their failures, can be observed by outside consultants as well as team members. Dyer's preferred approach to the problem is to have team members learn the difficult skills of "owning up, openness, and experimentation" so that individuality rather than conformity is fostered, as a result of concern for others rather than antagonism, and trust rather than distrust (Dyer, 1987:153).

In another chapter, Dyer considers several "people problems" in teams (1987:154-161). The people problems include:

1. When the boss is the major problem. Available solutions suggested by Dyer are laboratory training for the boss; gathering data about the manager's behavior from subordinates, interviews, or surveys; or having some member of the organization serve as an "honest observer."
2. Two-party conflicts. The two parties can meet privately, preferably with a consultant as a third party to work out the differences.
3. The problem member. If one member continually blocks the rest of the unit, Dyer suggests several possibilities. These are direct confrontation between the team leader and the problem person, confrontation by the group, giving the person a special responsibility to increase involvement, limiting the participation by asking the person to listen but not to speak and then have a one-to-one session with the leader, or by giving the person an external assignment.

4. Minority group members. If discrimination of any kind is present and directed towards a team member, Dyer recommends a special meeting to deal with the issue, if it is not dealt with in the course of normal group procedures.

Zander (1977:ch. 9) in his discussion of special problems outlines some assumptions underlying the recruiting and removal of group members. Gadon (1988) also suggests ways of helping a newcomer adjust to an ongoing work group.

Another set of hypotheses concerning the identification of various types of problem members and suggestions for overcoming the problems is presented by Bales (Bales & Cohen, 1979) in his discussion of the "dominant triangle" formed by the most active members of a group, those that are "far out" in relation to others, and those that may become scapegoats, mediators, or dominators. Bales also discusses the general tendency in groups to swing back and forth between unification and polarization.

Kanter (1983:256-264) identifies several "dilemmas of teamwork." In a well-functioning team, the contribution of individuals must be welcomed and valued. However four kinds of inequalities can prevent full participation:

1. Higher-status members may be given more time and their opinions given more weight.
2. People with more information about the task have an advantage over the others.
3. People bring to the team different levels of personal attractiveness, verbal skill, access to information networks, and interest in the task.
4. Outsiders or newcomers may feel uncomfortable about speaking up.

In addition there may be internal politics, a myth that everyone is now part of a "team" and it is not legitimate to acknowledge them or talk about them as individuals, and close bonds may develop between members so that it becomes difficult to be open and honest with one another.

Brown (1988) asks if group members have ROCS in their heads. The letters R, O, C, and S stand for four myths that can block effective teamwork:

1. Rationality: when there is in fact a large element of emotion.
2. Objectivity: when there is actually subjectivity.
3. Consciousness: when unconscious motivations are also present.
4. Separability: the idea that individuals make separate contributions when in fact one individual contribution is related to another and one team contribution related to other teams.

From his work with teams in the public sector, Golembiewski (1988) identifies seven social problems that do not appear to the same extent in business teams:

1. Fear and the slough of despond.
2. Frequent crises of agreement.
3. Prevalence of "loose coupling," in the form of unclear and overlapping sources of authority, or uncertainty about roles and priorities.
4. Dealing directly and constructively with power phenomena.
5. A relaxed approach to confidentiality.
6. The interface abhors "losers."
7. The press holds all the trump cards.

Other special problems that have been identified by consultants include the management of emotional expression (Bocialetti, 1988), gaps and overlapping in individual specialites (Colantvono & Schnidman, 1988), and racism and sexism (Miller, F., 1988).

EVALUATION

The methods of evaluation usually will be the same as those used in the initial diagnosis of the team's problems. If this is the first time the team has come together there also may be some team product that can be evaluated. If the team building is for a team that has been in existence for some time, then their effectiveness in decision making after the workshop can be compared with their effectiveness in decision making before. Parnell (1987) traces the failures of many team-building efforts to the unwillingness of the team members to perform self-examination in order to discover the conditions that prevent the unit from functioning as it was intended. As an aid to maintaining discipline within the team, Barkman (1987) recommends that teams "put performance on the line" by spelling out the consequences of failure to carry out the steps in a plan or by failure to reach objectives by the established time.

It is important for the team to receive "feedback" concerning the results of the evaluation (Pritchard, Jones, Roth, Stuebing & Ekeberg, 1988). Even without the extensive group dynamics literature on feedback, one might suppose that an individual or a team has a better chance of improving if problems can be identified and corrected (Hare, 1976; Hare, Blumberg, Davies & Kent, 1992). However Conlon and Barr (1989) warn that the feedback should be appropriate to the task. If the object is to give feedback about individual performance, then giving it as a group or in a highly social context may reduce its effectiveness by introducing unintended social comparisons. If a team is composed of persons of different nationalities, then it is better if the method used to collect data for evaluation and the method of feedback require little confrontation (Rigby, 1987).

NOTES

1. See also Burke, W. (1988); Hanson & Lubin (1988:80).

2. For a similar list see Weisbord (1988).

3. See also Boss & McConkie (1981); Eden (1985); Woodman & Sherwood (1980a, 1980b).

4. For additional examples of team-building interventions, see Beer, M. (1976); Beckhard (1966); George, W. (1977); and Marrow, Bowers, and Seashore (1967).

7
Team Building with SYMLOG

MARGARET COWEN

This case was selected because it presents an organizational approach to consulting and thereby encompasses many of the elements of team building and general consulting discussed in this book. Although not made explicit in the text of the chapter, if you review the elements discussed in Chapter 6 you will note that most, if not all, of the areas discussed are included in the description of the intervention presented here.

This particular case demonstrates the possibilities of intervening at the organizational, intergroup, group, and individual level simultaneously, using survey feedback to increase effectiveness on all of those levels, and using the feedback to build a management development program for ongoing training and retraining employees as they move through the organization. Although the company itself was small by some standards, the issues it was facing in terms of strategic growth, planned change, and future competitiveness are easily translatable to companies of virtually any size, and are appropriate for illustrative purposes.

INTRODUCTION

The SYMLOG Consulting Group was contacted in late spring 1987 by the president and CEO of a resort. He had been exposed to SYMLOG through an executive development program given at the Harvard Business School. There he had used SYMLOG's program for analyzing an individual's view of a team via a field diagram, called YOURVIEW. He was interested in knowing whether or not this technology was also available to teams working together.

In further discussion it turned out that his organization was growing rapidly, and he realized that in order to meet long-term growth projections for the organization, he would need a fully effective management team. He further understood that building strong teams throughout the organization would help the company realize its goals and increase the overall effectiveness and productivity of the total organization.

BACKGROUND

The organization was initially a small resort open only during the winter months. They had expanded dramatically during the last few years, with the goal of becoming a full-season resort and conference center. The president and a partner were the sole owners of the company, and they had begun implementing plans that included full lodging facilities for rent or time-share purchase, condominium units, and recreation activities of interest for many months of the year.

They leased out their food and beverage concessions, but maintained the staffing and housekeeping activities in all of the lodging facilities. The staff included about 40 full-time managers and supervisors, and about 100 full-time employees. Because the resort was still only fully operational in the winter season, there was a tremendous fluctuation in staffing requirements throughout the year. One of the goals in becoming a four-season resort was not only to stabilize revenues but also to level out some of this staffing requirement, so that more individuals hired could be guaranteed year-round employment. The organization was located in a somewhat isolated area, with a scarcity of available personnel. Hiring practices, benefits, salaries, and stability were therefore critical issues for job candidates. Job satisfaction became a necessity, as the hiring pool was limited and candidates had numerous options for employment in the area.

Another challenge for the organization was the wide range in education, job familiarity, and management practices within all levels of supervisory personnel. Job competence was quite high among the technical staff, and lower with those in the service aspects of the organization. Formal education was higher with those involved with the business and financial planning aspects of the organization, but not necessarily commensurate with skills and knowledge required for effective job performance. The organization had a value for management education, but had only recently begun to pursue a course of ongoing training for all managers and employees entering new jobs.

The mission of the organization centered around excellence. The mission statement was published in all of the company material for customers and staff. All of the employees had a good understanding of what the mission statement really meant, but were not in agreement as to how the future expansion plans would affect the mission and how they managed the business. During the hectic winter season, with part-time employees who had no investment in the organization or potential future as full-time employees, however, it was more difficult to transfer the operational definition of the mission into their work and interface with the public.

The management style of the company was similar to an extended family, not unlike many typical entrepreneurial organizations, and it became very important to maintain as much of those familial and close-knit working relationships among the staff as possible as the company grew. Therefore instead of hiring from without, the goal was to promote and train from within if feasible. It was not unusual to transfer employees from one area to another and allow them to learn the necessary technical job skills on the job. This enabled employees who aspired to management to see the possibility of upward mobility in the future and to train in a variety of positions along the way. Having an effective management development program and forums for ongoing training and feedback were critical to the overall strategic plan.

CONTRACTING

Initial conversations with the president focused around solidifying a common definition and understanding of team building and what that entails. It was agreed that in the initial week of meetings, scheduled to include all of the management staff, no problem solving would take place, only issues generation and values clarification. It was understood that by team building we were discussing the relationships of work team members with one another and the rest of the organization, and not the specific issues of how business is conducted. Through several conversations about the goals of the organization, SYMLOG Consulting Group (SCG) believed that building more effective teams throughout the organization would indeed be essential for the client company to realize its long-term strategy.

SCG's contract with the president was as follows:

1. Conduct a team-building session with the planning group of the management team.
2. Conduct a similar session with members of the planning group and their staffs.
3. Help identify isues of concern that need working over the next fifteen months.
4. Help design and implement a management development program for the organization that the company could train internally.
5. Establish a system whereby the organization could receive ongoing systematic feedback as to how well it was achieving its goals.
6. Conduct skill-building sessions as identified, or contract with others to do so.
7. Meet with management on a predetermined schedule throughout a fifteen-month period to assess present effectiveness and reassess next steps.
8. Train supervisors and employees in the same manner as the management staff, beginning sixty days from the initial intervention.

SCG believed that SYMLOG was the only tool available that could provide the framework for a project of this kind as it allows for the simultaneous examination of beliefs, values, and attitudes the individual holds regarding teamwork; the focal issues of power/authority, morale/ cohesion, standards/norms, and goals/objectives that are operative within and between teams; and the issues surrounding the desired future for the organization and its continued profitability and growth.

The client company had just undergone an extensive process of detailing a five-year strategic plan where some of their corporate priorities were reorganized, management needs assessed, ways of financing an increasing number of service facilities identified, methods for stabilizing their financial position defined, and priorities established around increasing the general attractiveness and accessibility of the area and increasing their competitive advantage. These and other strategies needed to be carefully developed and executed in the near future. The importance of having well-functioning teams that could receive ongoing and systematic feedback was clear.

DATA COLLECTION

The date for the initial intervention was set, and data were gathered from the participants well in advance of the meeting time. SYMLOG questionnaires were used in lieu of personal interviews with attendees. Because of the need to have baseline data against which the effectiveness of the intervention could be measured, several pieces of data were collected for the beginning session which would be repeated only at the end of the fifteen-month contracted time. Other questions were asked with each application of the SYMLOG rating form.

Participants were asked questions of relevance on the organizational, team, and individual level. They responded to questions on the Individual and Organizational Values form concerning the values embodied in the mission of the organization (code name MIS), values for teamwork shown in the current culture of the organization (CUR), values that would be needed in the future culture in order to be successful (FUT), values for teamwork they saw themselves and team members showing, and what values for teamwork they expected to be perceived as showing (EXP), wished to personally show (WSH), and rejected either in themselves or in others (REJ).

Results were computed and samples of those results are shown in figures throughout this chapter. All data were returned to the client groups and used as the basis for discussion and issue generation.

INITIAL MEETING

The first intervention with the organization occurred several months after the initial call. A number of memos had been exchanged and telephone conversations held, vitae of SYMLOG staff had been sent to the organization, and it had been determined that there was a good fit between the consultants' skills and the organization's needs. Four days were set aside to work with the top management/planning group and their respective work teams. The first two days were spent with the top planning group in the company, which was a mixture that crossed organizational lines but was essentially the steering committee for long-term projects. The next two days were spent with the entire management team, a group of about sixteen. Intact teams were present at that time.

The organizational data collected prior on mission, current culture, and future culture were used as a way of introducing the SYMLOG model to the client, both with the planning group during the first two days and then by the entire management team in the second two days. The organizational data also became the baseline against which the effectiveness of the entire intervention could be measured.

SCG staff worked first with the planning group because the leadership of the rest of the organization were members. They not only received feedback and examined data unique to their group, but also were trained sufficiently during the two-day intervention that they were able to act as facilitators to their own teams when they met on the third and fourth days with their subordinates.

These groups all had received previous management training, but personal and team feedback of the magnitude of SYMLOG was new for them. Experience with teamwork and the relevance for job performance varied among participants as well. The reporting structure (Table of Organization) was such that several individuals did not have a clearly defined team at the time of the first meeting. For this reason, the design of the first two two-day sessions with the management groups was critical in making the experience a positive and productive one, especially in light of the results which indicated several members within each of the various teams were polarized with other members.

DATA HANDBACK

The format of the initial meeting with the planning group was followed in the next two days with the management team, and in principle in each successive feedback meeting throughout the course of the fifteen months. Essentially, the organizational level data were shown first as a way of assessing (or reassessing) the situation, identifying areas of concern for all, and keeping the conversation on a more global level. It was from the organizational data that future training and development needs were identified and formed the basis for the ongoing management development program.

Aggregated group data were discussed next, again because it is less threatening and more comfortable generally to deal with, but also as a way of showing the group the many areas of convergence they had as individuals within the teams. The group data also were used as a way of targeting possible group norms that were operative and needed adjustment. The team was introduced to the notion that it is often easier to change a group by working through norms than by attempting to change one individual at a time. Group data also were used here before the individual data because polarizations within the team did exist and it is important not to move off group issues before the group takes ownership for the dynamics and problems inherent in the interpersonal functioning of the group. In general, once individual data appear, all hope of concentrating on strictly team issues evaporates.

Individual data were the last to be presented and discussed. Coaching sessions also were offered to each participant in every meeting in which they received personal feedback, and the formulation of individual development plans became part of the scope of the team-building process.

With each piece of survey feedback returned, members were first given the task of studying the data individually, then to work in dyads or triads as thinking clarifiers, and finally to share their thoughts in the larger group. This enabled more reticent members to have an opportunity to formulate their thinking privately and provided a structured forum whereby individuals could share their thoughts according to their own comfort level.

SYMLOG was used as way of presenting the client group with systematic feedback and a method of discussing various issues while using a common language. The theory initially was not important, and only as much SYMLOG theory as was necessary—about a ten-minute introduction—was given in order to have participants undertand the feedback that was being returned. However, in later meetings, learning more about observing and categorizing behavior became important, and the actual focus of the developmental meeting was on better learning the SYMLOG model and language.

On an organizational level, the data established the framework for future work and the similarity with which members saw the needed future. The data were used on the group level to facilitate discussions about group norms and provide a way of beginning to change some of the more dysfunctional norms in the teams. On the individual level, the data provided benchmarks by which individuals could form personal development plans.

MEETING DESIGN—TWO-DAY TEAM BUILDING WITH THE PLANNING GROUP

Because many participants had not received indepth feedback from coworkers before, a warm-up exercise was used to help the group become comfortable with looking at their own behavior and giving and receiving feedback. The Interpersonal Effectiveness Profile is a self-report, self-scoring instrument that introduces the concept of a "norm" and helps establish a mind-set as to the kinds of discussions that can take place once individual feedback was returned. They were introduced to the field diagram and the three-dimensional space by reviewing diagrams of "famous people" plotted on a diagram, and by looking at the "scatter plots" of the organizational images they rated prior to the meeting.

The next thing we did was look at each individual's view of the group. After they saw the scatters on the organization they were given their individual data so that they could see what kinds of potential polarizations they saw in the group, how unified the group was as far as they were concerned, and where they themselves expected to be seen vis-a-vis the rest of the group. A report was generated to accompany the field diagram, and work was accomplished by looking at the issues of leadership and its relationship to each individual's placement of images in a personal field diagram. Discussion was around how to personally modify behavior with certain individuals in order to better meet their needs and therefore the needs of a more unified team.

They were then taken through an exercise where they were asked to focus on teamwork effectiveness, and by using a blank bar graph construct their own personal norm for effectiveness, and categorize the twenty-six items into those that contribute to effective teamwork, are sometimes necessary but dangerous to effective teamwork, and almost always interfere with teamwork. Individuals worked alone, then shared with a partner, and then shared within their entire team. Subgroups reported out, and the similarities of all findings led to a general discussion of team effectiveness and the concept that all behaviors do not necessarily help teamwork and can be either over-or underemphasized in the optimal. Issues of team membership and leadership followed, and the more important aspects of what is a team and why is teamwork important were raised and discussed openly.

That introduction allowed us to show the bar graph on the aggregated data for the group as a whole. They had rated the values for teamwork they believed each individual showed, and those data were placed into both bar graph and field diagram formats. The bar graph had an extensive report associated with it which members were asked to read individually before sharing thoughts within the larger group. They were asked to make a list of items that were surprising to them and where they thought the bar graph showed values that contributed to effective teamwork. They were then divided into groups of three to discuss their observations on the group.

A large general discussion then took place. The data were shown to the group on a transparency using an overhead projector. These discussions were facilitated by the consultant. The bar graph was used as a means of looking at the future development needs of the group. When the norms had been identified and discussed, the group average field diagram was shown. The group average field diagram indicates how each member was rated on average by the group, and each member's relative location to others and to the concepts of the group wish and reject. Seeing the diagram helped facilitate a discussion of group dynamics, how the group constellation relates to the norms of the group, and what roles people appeared to be playing in the group. From this discussion individual change can begin, with the support and acknowledgement that unification is a team goal.

Figure 7.1 represents the group average perspective of the planning group on the major concepts. The images of team members are shown without identifiers, though all circles were labeled during the intervention. In general, the group was less positive and more inflexible and rule-oriented than they wanted to be (as evidenced by the group wish image). There was quite a bit of difference in the circle sizes of some of the images, indicating a

Figure 7.1
Ratings on Each Other and Organizational Concepts, at Initial Intervention

Values on Accepting Task-Orientation of Established Authority

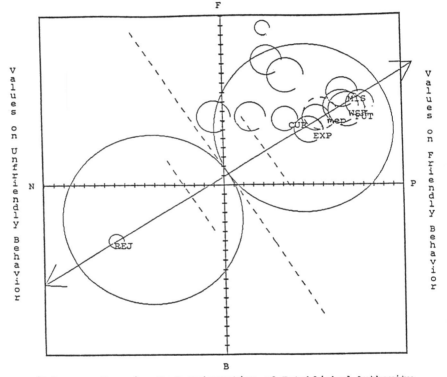

Values on Opposing Task-Orientation of Established Authority

Source: SYMLOG Consulting Group, San Diego, CA. Field diagram copyright © 1983 by R. F. Bales. Reprinted by permission of SYMLOG Consulting Group.

Notes: Larger circle diameters indicate increased dominance.
Expansion multiplier = 1.47
CUR = current culture; MIS = Mission of the organization;
FUT = desired future culture; mep = "benchmark profile";
EXP = expect self to be seen by others; WSH = wish to show; REJ = reject;
B = backward; F = forward; N = negative; P = positive

potential polarization on the dominant-submissive dimension, and one member was seen on average in the negative part of the space.

The final piece was handing back data on how the group viewed each member individually. They were asked to carefully read and study the data individually and determine what they were doing both to contribute to and detract from the team effectiveness. They were then asked to pair with another person and in light of the data formulate answers to the questions, "what was surprising to you that you need to have clarified," "what pleased you that the group sees you as contributing," and "what would you like to modify with which you want group help." A group discussion was conducted, and the discussion took a general turn where they talked with one another almost three hours. Individuals were able to elicit answers to questions they had, and thereby become more comfortable with their data and develop plans on how to become more effective.

This individual bar graph and report information was welcomed for the most part, as the design had led each member to realize that any problems that the teams were having had to be solved by the team, and that no one person was at fault or to blame for any problems that were occurring. It had further been stressed that it was the goal and responsibility of the group, in conjunction with any individual, to work together to unify the team, and no individual would be without group support for any changes he or she might wish to make. So support was clearly available to anyone wishing to modify his or her behavior based on feedback from the team.

At that point the discussion was tied back to the organizational data to see if there were any common threads in the organizational data that showed up on the individual bar graphs. They started a tentative list of organizational issues. The consultants made themselves available for a one-hour meeting to answer questions on a personal level with any of the individuals as they prepared to go into a meeting with their subordinates during the next two days.

TWO-DAY MEETING—ALL-MANAGEMENT GROUP

The next two days with the entire management team were designed to mirror the sequence used with the management group. However the leader was able to answer some of the queries, help facilitate the small group discussions, and was receiving yet additional feedback. The feedback to the planning group had been peer group. The feedback that the planning group members then received for the next two days was from their intact team (their subordinates), and the team leaders had the additional job of reconciling and accounting for any differences in the two sets of data. Most of them chose to share their two sets of data with their work teams and help work through any differences with their subordinates.

One of the reasons for having the managers as actively involved as possible in the meetings was that one of the intended outcomes of the team building and the entire development process was to move the group ahead so that they could function without a consultant. The goal was for the organization to have self-monitoring teams with the use of systematic feedback on a fairly regular basis. It was hoped that they would have achieved a skill level to allow them to work with one another in such a way that they could monitor their own processes and outcomes and do so on an ongoing basis.

Members of the management team saw the values embodied in the current organizational culture quite differently, which is detailed in Figure 7.1. In Figure 7.2, each of the circles represents one rating by a management team member. There is quite a variance, not only in the size of the circles (i.e., the level of dominance individuals perceive in the current culture), but also whether or not the culture embodies values that oppose the established authority or accept the established authority, almost without question. These different perceptions would be disturbing, except that the group's view of the needed future culture, in order to be most effective, was quite a bit more similar (see Figure 7.3). Although some variance remains in the group's view of the future in Figure 7.3, all images fall within one quadrant, and some of the extreme positions between the top half of the diagram (toward the F) and the bottom half have been modified. These results would at least indicate that members have a similar enough view of the future to be able to act in concert to make the future a reality.

To facilitate and clarify a discussion on teams and the kinds of teams that exist in business, the distinction was made between a bunch, a group, and a team, teams being those constellations who are interdependent and share a common goal and purpose. The concept of teams was further clarified by using degree of specialization and need for coordination as factors that help to determine the kind of team with which you are working. The greater the degree of specialization within team members, and the greater the need for coordination, the greater the need for effective teamwork and time to plan, organize, and develop collaborative strategies together.

The conclusions of the teams was that there was a great deal of difference between what the accounting department did and what the housekeeping department did in terms of their need to get the job done. The interface between some of the teams, the rest of the organization, and the clients was also important since some teams worked primarily with other resources within the organization and some teams worked primarily with the outside guests. That distinction helped all teams recognize their special need for meeting together and sharing information between and among the teams.

Dyads and triads were used extensively over the course of the four days as thinking clarifiers, to provide an opportunity for the more reticent members to talk personally with someone before they shared in the larger group, and to gain some comfort and acceptance with the feedback. The second session

Figure 7.2
Perceptions of Current Culture, at Initial Intervention

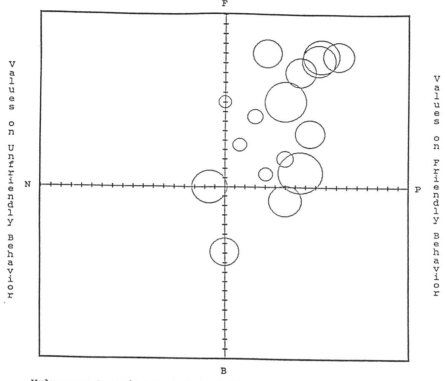

Values on Accepting Task-Orientation of Established Authority

Values on Opposing Task-Orientation of Established Authority

Source: SYMLOG Consulting Group, San Diego, CA. Field diagram copyright © 1983 by
    R. F. Bales. Reprinted by permission of SYMLOG Consulting Group.

Notes: Larger circle diameters indicate increased dominance.
    Potential expansion multiplier between 1.00 and 1.50.
    B = backward; F = forward; N = negative; P = positive

with the management team was the first time that some of them had ever
received feedback, although they had gone through quite a bit of management development prior to that time.

CONSIDERATIONS

One of SCG's concerns was the difference in educational levels and back-
grounds of the client organization, and whether or not SYMLOG would be

Figure 7.3
Desired Future Culture, at Initial Intervention

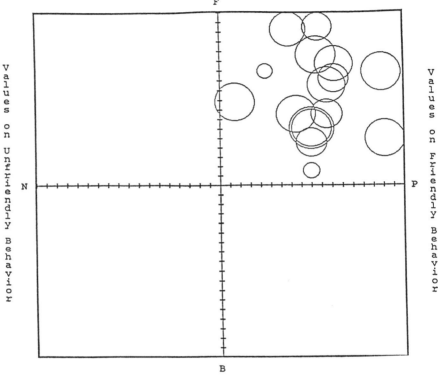

Values on Accepting Task-Orientation of Established Authority

Values on Opposing Task-Orientation of Established Authority

Source: SYMLOG Consulting Group, San Diego, CA. Field diagram copyright © 1983 by R. F. Bales. Reprinted by permission of SYMLOG Consulting Group.

Notes: Larger circle diameters indicate increased dominance.
Potential expansion multiplier between 1.00 and 1.50.
B = backward; F = forward; N = negative; P = positive

an equally appropriate tool for all of them. The wording of the twenty-six-item questionnaire was thought by others to be potentially problematic. We had individuals in the room with no more than an eighth-grade education, and some with postdoctoral education.

As it turned out, neither the language of the items nor the concept of three-dimensional space was a problem for any of the individuals. Team members were asked to give specific behavioral examples of what an individual might have been doing that led them to be perceived and rated as they were. Team members had no difficulty at all telling one another what they were thinking about when they made their ratings.

It previously had been determined that the meetings would include issues generation, and not problem solving as well, so the next steps had to be completed prior to disbanding. The organizational data served in both meetings as the catalyst for future work. Each team made its own internal assignments, and the larger management team decided they wanted to pursue management development together. A list of needed topics was given to SCG, and they were requested to draft a proposed development schedule for the future fifteen months. Systematic feedback was to be part of the ongoing training, and placed into each of the future development modules as appropriate.

Supervisory training was to be done in conjunction with the management development work. Supervisors were to have abridged versions of each of the management level training, and some training needs specific to their supervisory work. SCG also was requested to find and train a supervisory program that would meet the specific client needs and be integrated with the overall scope of the development project just begun.

SCG consultants wrote a summary for the president, and the proposal was adopted and work begun two months after the initial meetings. The management development program would follow the traditional schema known as PLOC: planning, leading, organizing, and controlling. The piece on leading and leadership would be highlighted in all meetings. The skills that managers thought they needed revolved around planning, organizing, and controlling. So the theme for future sessions would first focus on planning, then organizing, then controlling. The consistent theme throughout all of these was their SYMLOG feedback.

The topics to examine were ones targeted by the group from the bar graph and the current culture (CUR) report, which they studied during the two-day meeting (see Figure 7.4). The current culture bar graph looked almost identical to their group average bar graph, and better highlighted the areas the group agreed were problematic and needed attention.

The group noted the underemphasis shown in the bar graph on items dealing with planning, collaboration, and the use of information and how it was communicated. It was in these areas that they wished to begin their development training.

FIRST FOLLOW-UP MEETING

The first follow-up meeting was three days long, held two months after the initial set of meetings. The agenda was effective meeting skills. All management team members were involved. Traditional meeting information was shared, and the primary model of instruction used was Theory, Demonstration, Practice, Action (TDPA). SYMLOG feedback was collected using the

Figure 7.4
Current Perceptions of Management Members, at Initial Meeting

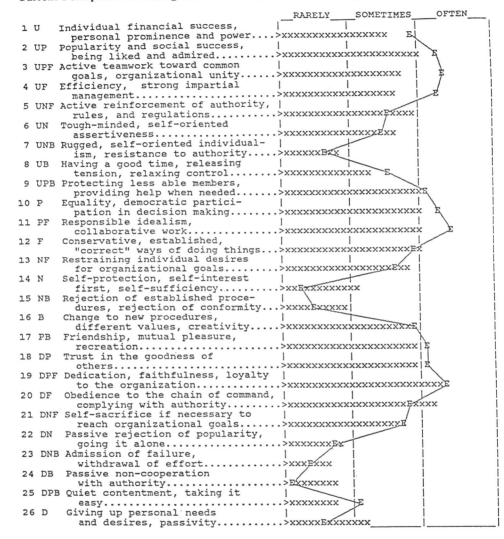

```
                                          RARELY____SOMETIMES____OFTEN___
 1 U   Individual financial success,      |        |          |
       personal prominence and power....>xxxxxxxxxxxxxxxxxxx   E|
 2 UP  Popularity and social success,     |        |          |
       being liked and admired..........>xxxxxxxxxxxxxxxxxxxxxx  E
 3 UPF Active teamwork toward common      |        |          |
       goals, organizational unity......>xxxxxxxxxxxxxxxxxxxx  |   E
 4 UF  Efficiency, strong impartial       |        |          |
       management.......................>xxxxxxxxxxxxxxxxxx    |   E
 5 UNF Active reinforcement of authority, |        |          |
       rules, and regulations...........>xxxxxxxxxxxxxxxxxxxExxxx|
 6 UN  Tough-minded, self-oriented        |        |          |
       assertiveness....................>xxxxxxxxxxxxxxxxxxExx    |
 7 UNB Rugged, self-oriented individual-  |        |          |
       ism, resistance to authority.....>xxxxxxxBxx |          |
 8 UB  Having a good time, releasing      |        |          |
       tension, relaxing control........>xxxxxxxxxxxxxxx  E    |
 9 UPB Protecting less able members,      |        |          |
       providing help when needed.......>xxxxxxxxxxxxxxxxxxxxxxxxE
10 P   Equality, democratic partici-      |        |          |
       pation in decision making........>xxxxxxxxxxxxxxxxxxxxxx  E
11 PF  Responsible idealism,              |        |          |
       collaborative work...............>xxxxxxxxxxxxxxxxxxxxxx  |  E
12 F   Conservative, established,         |        |          |
       "correct" ways of doing things...>xxxxxxxxxxxxxxxxxxxExx  |
13 NF  Restraining individual desires     |        |          |
       for organizational goals.........>xxxxxxxxxxxxxxxxxExx   |
14 N   Self-protection, self-interest     |        |          |
       first, self-sufficiency..........>xxExxxxxxxxxx |        |
15 NB  Rejection of established proce-     |        |          |
       dures, rejection of conformity...>xxxxExxxxx|            |
16 B   Change to new procedures,          |        |          |
       different values, creativity.....>xxxxxxxxxxxxxxxxxxxxxxxE|
17 PB  Friendship, mutual pleasure,       |        |          |
       recreation.......................>xxxxxxxxxxxxxxxxxxxxxx|E
18 DP  Trust in the goodness of           |        |          |
       others...........................>xxxxxxxxxxxxxxxxxxxxxx|E
19 DPF Dedication, faithfulness, loyalty  |        |          |
       to the organization..............>xxxxxxxxxxxxxxxxxxxxxxxxxxxxE
20 DF  Obedience to the chain of command, |        |          |
       complying with authority.........>xxxxxxxxxxxxxxxxxxxxxExxxx
21 DNF Self-sacrifice if necessary to     |        |          |
       reach organizational goals.......>xxxxxxxxxxxxxxxxxxxxxE
22 DN  Passive rejection of popularity,   |        |          |
       going it alone...................>xxxxxxxExx |          |
23 DNB Admission of failure,              |        |          |
       withdrawal of effort.............>xxxExxxx  |          |
24 DB  Passive non-cooperation            |        |          |
       with authority...................>Exxxxxxxx |          |
25 DPB Quiet contentment, taking it       |        |          |
       easy.............................>xxxxxxxxx |E         |
26 D   Giving up personal needs           |        |          |
       and desires, passivity...........>xxxxxExxxxxxx____     |____
```

Source: SYMLOG Consulting Group, San Diego, CA. Copyright © 1983 by R. F. Bales. Reprinted by permission of SYMLOG Consulting Group.

Notes: Type: PF; Final Location: 2U 4P 4F; Number of Raters: 16

     E = optimum location for most effective; x = the average rating on each item;

     B = backward; D = downward; F = forward; N = negative; P = positive;

     U = upward

Behavior Form instead of the Individual and Organizational Value items. This allowed individuals to begin to focus on the specific behaviors others were seeing and evaluating, and possible ways of bringing into better alignment their intended behavior with what was being observed. The SYMLOG model was used as a way of teaching behavior observation skills, and participants were asked to practice a variety of behaviors, many of which seemed foreign and difficult to them initially.

One of the reasons for starting with effective meetings was that some of the managers were having meetings irregularly with their subordinates who were supervisors, and some managers were not having meetings of their team at all. In those cases where meetings were held, comments indicated the meetings were too long, unfocused, boring, and could as well be handled with a well-written memo. Managers who did attend meetings were passing information downward to their subordinates in a scanty fashion, if at all, and never via a well-planned and well-attended staff meeting. If teams were to become important, the management group rightly felt that team meetings were essential and needed to be of as high a quality as possible.

This session looked not only at how to conduct an effective meeting but also at how to be an effective group member in a meeting. The discrimination was made between process and content, managing the task functions versus the group maintenance functions. Group roles were discussed and behaviors practiced. Communication skills, such as active listening, were part of the two days. When the feedback on their behaviors was returned, the data were used as a means of increasing their effectiveness at the behavioral level and teaching them to be better observers of behavior. The better they would be able to observe, the better they would be able to act intentionally.

One of the concepts in the year-long program, unlike other interventions with SYMLOG, was that SYMLOG was to become an operative model for these people so that they would be able to use the model itself and not merely benefit from the feedback. In the two days spent on effective meetings, we were very explicit about parts of the three-dimensional SYMLOG space. We "taught" the space intentionally, instead of merely using SYMLOG as a method of introducing the feedback as we had in the first set of meetings. Participants discussed how they would intervene in organizations. We put the group in "fish bowls" so that they had to live out what various scenarios would be like, and then brainstorm alternative ways of responding to comments and situations.

As practice for an effective meeting, we took them through a problem-solving meeting which was very much related to their selection needs for the upcoming winter months. We developed a selection system for them that would not be dependent upon a computer but that they could use as a quick way to assess the potential of some of the candidates. Because they had a limited pool from which to hire, they were looking more for a method of screening out those individuals who would clearly be unacceptable and potentially dangerous to the work force than they were to screening in good management candidates or individuals whom they would want to hire as permanent yearly employees. After the grueling winter season, and a sixty-day trial period, they planned to have subordinates and/or co-workers complete SYMLOG ratings on the individual as part of the permanent hiring procedure.

SECOND FOLLOW-UP MEETING

Supervisory training was begun four months after the initial management meetings. Supervisors had a minimal introduction to SYMLOG, but were asked to rate several organizational concepts, themselves, and their team members. Personal feedback from their subordinates was not part of the meeting, but with their own view of the group they did have an introduction to group dynamics.

The supervisory training was to teach some of the basics of management, as well as highlight the critical training points from each of the management team's training sessions. The structure of planning and conducting a good meeting were reviewed with the supervisors, and they also attended two half days of basic supervisory training.

THIRD FOLLOW-UP MEETING

Three months later, in early spring of the next year, the supervisors had their second meeting, in what was the third follow-up meeting for the company. They received feedback from their subordinates on how they were perceived to behave, in general, and what they could do to be more effective in the eyes of the subordinates. The introduction to the supervisors, because they had not ever received feedback, was meant to be merely introductory. The session was designed to minimize the intensity; supervisors were not in attendance with their intact teams and received ratings on behaviors, not the underlying teamwork values data which are richer but generally more threatening to a naive audience.

The focus of the training was on the supervisor and the work team. The subordinates were hourly employees for the most part, and many were not highly motivated. The two half days of basic training they received were merely a continuation of what was started three months earlier, and focused on making job assignments and tracking problem employees. At that time, because of cost considerations and travel by the consultants, the supervisory training always was coupled with the management team training.

The management team meeting revolved around time management, another issue that had come out of the first session. In addition to time management, the managers also were guided through a work audit to include what they were doing currently, what subordinates were doing currently, what was being done that no longer needed doing, and what was not being done that should be started. Accountabilities were also at issue. The organization was not unlike many small organizations where promotion was from within, where the "doers" became the managers of the work. Many of the managers were still doing things that their subordinates could have done. Several had changed departments during the period of growth and there was duplication of effort in some of the areas.

The work audit was conducted in such a way that each individual worked on his or her own job. His or her boss was in the room as well. So the workers then had to talk with their bosses and the departments had to talk with one another. The overall boss was also in the room. With that kind of structure, we made some major progress in where overlaps were and what kinds of things could be given to subordinates and what kinds of things need not continue to be done. Some things had always been done that way and no one had ever taken a look at the distribution of work. There was no direct SYMLOG feedback during these two days, as the focus was entirely on the organizing portion of the planning, leading, organizing, and controlling.

FOURTH FOLLOW-UP MEETING

Ten months after the beginning of the intervention, the supervisors received their last supervisory training. As they were dealing with issues in the subsequent session from the management team, the supervisors worked on breaking down their jobs into activities that could be standardized and for which performance criteria could be developed.

The entire organization made SYMLOG ratings again on the culture data. Participants responded to the question, "What kinds of values are currently shown in the culture of the organization?" and "What kinds of values need to be shown in the future in order to be most effective?"

As everyone had hoped, the training and conversations had opened up the possibility for a different type of future, and an environment where the "current" culture felt quite different to people than ten months earlier. Change had indeed started, along with the pure acquisition of skills that occurs during the didactic part of training.

Figure 7.5 is a group average field diagram of the management team's aggregated responses to the questions regarding current (CUR) and future (FUT) culture in the organization. Both are moving in an effective direction and appear to indicate the management team members are feeling more empowered. Figure 7.6 shows the variance with which current culture was rated. Of note here is that the current culture seems much more cohesive than earlier, more positive, and more influential. In short, most members hold a very similar and positive view of the current culture. Figure 7.7 also shows variance, but this time the ratings are on the future culture needed in

Figure 7.5
Aggregate on Current and Desired Future Cultures, at the End of Ten Months

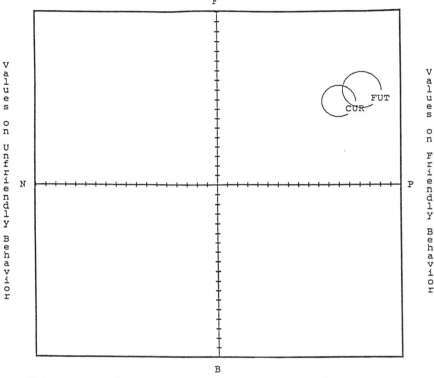

Values on Accepting Task-Orientation of Established Authority

Values on Opposing Task-Orientation of Established Authority

Source: SYMLOG Consulting Group, San Diego, CA. Copyright © 1983 by R. F. Bales.
    Reprinted by permission of SYMLOG Consulting Group.

Notes: Larger circle diameters indicate increased dominance.
    Expansion multiplier = 1.50
    B = backward; F = forward; N = negative; P = positive

order to be most effective. Again, the ratings are quite similar and have
shifted in a more positive, cohesive direction.

For the skill training portion of the meetings, we worked with the managers
on the controlling part of PLOC. We went through quality controls, setting
up standards, and performance management. By this time SYMLOG was
used to demonstrate how problems in this area were directly attributable to
the low "Forward" items in the bar graphs. What was needed was to be
able to monitor and delegate in such a way that time was freed up but the
work would still be done.

Figure 7.6
Current Culture, at the End of Ten Months

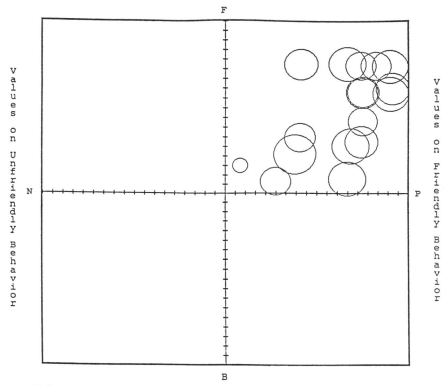

Values on Accepting Task-Orientation of Established Authority

Values on Opposing Task-Orientation of Established Authority

Source: SYMLOG Consulting Group, San Diego, CA. Copyright © 1983 by R. F. Bales.
Reprinted by permission of SYMLOG Consulting Group.

Notes: Larger circle diameters indicate increased dominance.
Potential expansion multiplier between 1.00 and 1.50.
B = backward; F = forward; N = negative; P = positive

FINAL MEETING

The final meeting was fifteen months after the initial session, and was meant to be a review of the entire team-building venture. One day was spent outlining and reviewing the major learning points from the previous sessions.

It was the first time that the supervisors were not in session to learn skills, but heading up their intact team in a facilitative capacity. The supervisors and their direct employees embarked on the team-building session that had first brought SCG together with the client organization fifteen months

Figure 7.7
Desired Future Culture, at the End of Ten Months

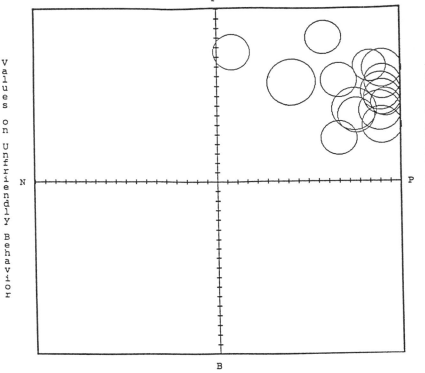

Values on Accepting Task-Orientation of Established Authority

Values on Opposing Task-Orientation of Established Authority

Source: SYMLOG Consulting Group, San Diego, CA. Copyright © 1983 by R. F. Bales.
Reprinted by permission of SYMLOG Consulting Group.

Notes: Larger circle diameters indicate increased dominance.
Potential expansion multiplier between 1.00 and 1.50.
B = backward; F = forward; N = negative; P = positive

before, and the management team was present to act as coaches and consultants to the supervisors.

The planning group met separately again for a one-day session, prior to meeting with the management team. The constellation of the team was considerably more unified, and in general the team felt the development effort was successful. The team also felt the needed skills had been transferred internally as was originally hoped and felt confident they could carry forth the effort with a minimum of outside help. Figure 7.8 shows the group

Figure 7.8
Team Member Ratings on Each Other, at Final Intervention
(Fourteen Months after Initial Intervention)

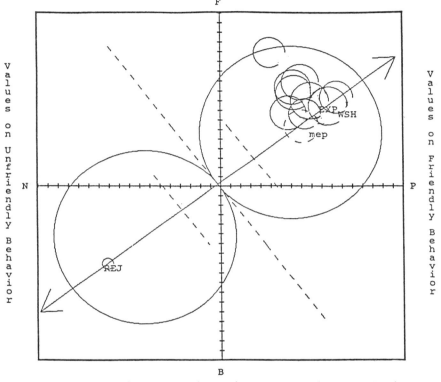

Values on Accepting Task-Orientation of Established Authority

Values on Opposing Task-Orientation of Established Authority

Source: SYMLOG Consulting Group, San Diego, CA. Copyright © 1983 by R. F. Bales.
Reprinted by permission of SYMLOG Consulting Group.

Notes: Larger circle diameters indicate increased dominance.
Expansion multiplier = 1.20
EXP = expect self to be seen by others; mep = "benchmark profile";
REJ = reject; WSH = wish to show; B = backward; F = forward; N = negative;
P = positive

average constellation of the planning group fourteen months after they
began their serious team-building and management development effort.
The group average bar graph is included as Figure 7.9.

The team looked very healthy on paper, and felt collaborative and
cohesive. They had learned to deal constructively with conflict and to

Figure 7.9
Planning Group, Combined Ratings, at Final Intervention
(Fourteen Months after Initial Intervention)

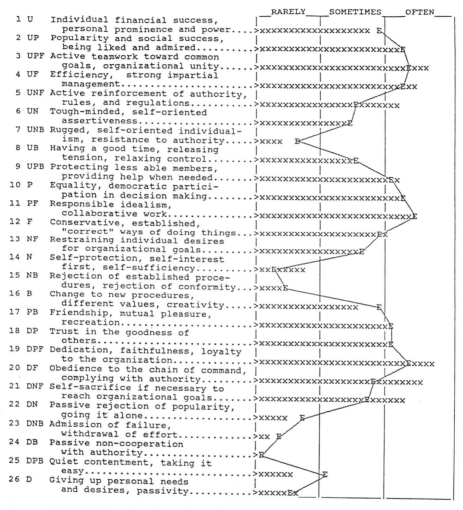

Notes: Type: UPF; Final Location: 4U 6P 8F; Number of Raters: 7

E = optimum location for most effective; x = the average rating on each item;
B = backward; D = downward; F = forward; N = negative; P = positive;
U = upward

discuss differences of opinion and strategy openly. The process had been difficult for all at times, and one of the members was no longer on the team. But the general feeling of the group was one that the effort was worthwhile and that they would never have been successful and able to move forward without having taken the time to establish the ongoing feedback and education process.

The management team made a set of SYMLOG ratings on the Individual and Organizational Values each member showed in his or her behavior, and spent one day with the data reviewing progress and refining development plans. The results of their efforts looked very similar to the planning group. As an entire team, they looked back at the last year to see how well they had institutionalized the team-building skills and where they needed to go in the future. They had been monitoring an established quality control system after each of the meetings. The planning team and the management team had continued to move ahead with a great many of the programs that were discussed. Those were now in place with many new ideas on the drawing board.

The supervisors were beginning the process with the management team guiding their efforts. Clearly systematic feedback is necessary to know if you are on target and moving in the appropriate direction. In this instance, SYMLOG was the method we used to guide the intervention and become institutionalized to help the organization reach into the future and become the best that it could be.

PART II
THEORIES OF SOCIAL INTERACTION AND APPLICATIONS

8
Functional Analysis

A brief introduction to functional theory has been given in Chapter 1, including a description of the four basic functions that any group must fulfill in order to survive, an indication of the order in which these functions usually are dealt with as a group develops, and the fact that the four functions form a "cybernetic hierarchy." The present chapter provides a summary outline of aspects of the theory, especially as it applies to groups and teams. (For a more detailed presentation, including illustrative figures and tables, see Hare, 1983a.)

FOUR FUNCTIONAL CATEGORIES

Functional theory was developed by Parsons and his colleagues with a primary focus on large social systems (Parsons, 1961; Effrat, 1968; Loubser et al., 1976). The four functions are: (L) the members of the group must share a common identity and be committed to the values of the group; (A) they must have or be able to generate the skills and resources necessary to reach the group goal; (I) they must have rules that allow them to coordinate their activity and enough feeling of solidarity to stay together to complete the task, and (G) they must be able to exercise enough control over their membership to coordinate the use of resources and member roles in pursuit of their common goal.

The descriptions of the functional categories have been introduced in the order in which they would appear as phases in the development of a group. In the literature on functional analysis, the four categories usually are referred to by the first letters of the names of the categories as AGIL. The formal names of the categories are: Adaptation, Goal-attainment, Integration, and Latent pattern maintenance and tension management.

The relatively long title of the "L" sector contains several ideas. The central idea is that every group needs a set of values and a pattern of activity that must be maintained if the group is to have integrity. The term "latent" appears because most groups meet only occasionally, then the group is "manifest." The members' commitment to the basic values must be strong enough to carry them over the periods when they are not meeting face to face. The idea of "tension management" is included in the L sector because too much tension, associated with the failure of work in any area, can throw a group back to "square one" and cast doubt on the meaning of the activity. Thus tension must be managed before the group can return to work.

In a large social system, such as a nation, the four categories (AGIL) are represented by the economic, political, legal, and familial and religious sub-structures. For each of these areas there is a generalized medium of exchange (in the order A,G,I,L: money, power, influence, and commitments), a value principle that guides action in this area (utility, effectiveness, solidarity, and integrity), and a standard of coordination for activity (solvency, success, consensus, and pattern consistency).

An activity that seems to be primarily *economic*, such as raising money to be used for the general purposes of the group, where the focus is on utility with a concern for solvency, would be classified in the A or *adaptive* sector. An activity that seems religious or familial, concerned with basic commitments to the group, its integrity, and the consistency of its pattern over time, would be classified in the L or *pattern maintenance* sector. Other activities would be classified as *integration* or *goal-attainment* according to the criteria indicated above. Andrew Effrat has provided a set of categories for identifying activity in each of these four areas in a small group (Hare, 1982: 25; Hare, 1983a: 432).

THE CYBERNETIC HIERARCHY OF CONTROL

The "cybernetic hierarchy of control" is a concept that was first applied to the analysis of physical systems, but it can be applied to social systems as well. The basic assumption is that a part of a system containing *information* will be able to control a part of a system containing *energy*. The standard examples for physical systems are the room thermostat that processes information about temperature and is able to control a source of heat or cooling and a computer that controls an industrial production line (Effrat, 1976:666-669).

In a social system, the four functions also form a cybernetic hierarchy. The area of pattern maintenance (L) controls the integrative area (I), which in turn provides more control than the goal-attainment area (G). The adaptive area (A) is at the bottom of the hierarchy.

GROUP DEVELOPMENT

Groups tend to develop in four phases, as indicated previously, in the sequence L-A-I-G, with a terminal stage of L when the group is disbanded.

In the terminal stage the group redefines the relationships between members and the group, distributes the remaining resources, and considers the meaning of the group experience for the individual member. This sequence was suggested by Effrat and tested in an analysis of a small regional development board in the Philippines (Hare, 1968), by comparison with other theories (Hare, 1973), and elaborated on the basis of experience in Curacao, Netherlands Antilles (Hare & Blumberg, 1977:281-282).

The amount of time the group spends in each phase is determined by the activity of the leader (by direction or lack of direction) and the skills and emotional strengths of the members. The leader may be ready for each phase at the outset if the leader is chosen because of experience with this type of group. However, members come to a group with different degrees of problem-solving skills and preferences for different emotional modalities. Subgroups tend to form on the basis of skills and emotional modalities. If the subgroup with the appropriate skills and emotional state is large enough or strong enough, it can carry the whole group through a phase. If not enough members of the group are ready for a particular phase, more intervention by the leader may be necessary. Some groups never progress beyond the early phases and some recycle through the same phase several times before gaining enough closure on that phase to move on to the next. In general, the functional needs of a given phase must be met before the group is ready to move on to the next phase (cf. Bennis & Shepard, 1956:420; Schutz, 1958:171; Mills, 1964:78).

PHASES WITHIN PHASES

It may be enough to identify the basic four phases of group development (L-A-I-G) with a terminal phase of L for many purposes, however it is also possible to identify the sequence of four subphases within each of the major phases. This provides a better understanding of how a group moves from one phase to another as well as integrating the observations of Shambaugh (1978) on emotionality and task activity in groups (Hare, 1983a:437-439).

The subphases within phases are most easily seen when the group requires some special equipment and when the nature of the work requires clear role differentiation. This can be illustrated with an example from the voyage of the raft *Acali* from the coast of Africa to the coast of Mexico in 1972 (Genovés, 1979; see also Hare, 1974; Hare, 1983a:434-437). Santiago Genovés, who organized the raft voyage, had been a member of two voyages on papyrus rafts led by Thor Heyerdahl (1972) over the same route. Among the many differences in the purposes and equipment of the voyages, Santiago had deduced that his raft should be unsinkable.

The activity of building and equipping the raft can be used as an example of the phases within phases in the adaptive area. Part of this activity was completed in England where the raft had been designed and built before being shipped to Las Palmas where the crew was assembled. However a distinct A phase was required to complete the work and prepare the raft for the sea voyage. This involved a whole set of ideas for construction and provisions (subphase L of A), special tools to be acquired or improvised (subphase A of A), ship's carpenters and other specialized roles (subphase I of A), and the work of outfitting the raft (subphase G of A). Subphases also could be identified within the L, I, G, and terminal L phases.

During the course of a group's development, some persons may drop out—perhaps at the end of the L phase if they are not satisfied with the overall goals of the group. Others may be satisfied with the goals but drop out at the end of the A phase if they judge that resources, especially funds, are not adequate. However the "revolution within the revolution" is most likely to occur near the end of the I phase if some members are dissatisfied with the leadership or the role distribution. By this time they have become committed to the idea of the group and the resources seem to be adequate. Thus if change does not occur at this point, there is nothing left to do but carry on the work.

PRESSURES TO CONFORM

For the analysis of the pressures on individuals to conform in groups, the theories of Jahoda (1956) and Kelman (1958) suggest reasons why different types of variables might have different effects (Hare, 1983a:439-442). Their work in turn can be understood in terms of the four functional categories and the cybernetic hierarchy. For example, one can urge conformity on the basis of common values (L), for the sake of friendship (I), because a majority or someone in authority dominates the scene (G), or because of the facts of the case (A). From the cybernetic hierarchy, one would expect L variables to be the most persuasive and A variables to be the least persuasive. Values (L), once internalized, will be the hardest to change, next are norms (I), represented by reciprocal role relationships and the impact of reference groups, that are effective as long as the norms are salient. Next comes the power of the majority or an authority (G) that is effective only under the conditions of surveillance, and last comes the influence of facts or funds (A) that are only effective at the time of the exchange.

Unfortunately, few experiments consider more than one variable at a time, so it is difficult to find supporting evidence that the four types of pressures toward conformity are ordered according to the L, I, G, A hierarchy. Kelman's (1958) experiment demonstrates that variables of the L, I, and G types have an influence on attitude change (see also Leet-Pellegrini & Rubin, 1974). Experiments by Kiesler and colleagues give evidence that commitment to continue in a group (L) is a more powerful influence on conformity than attraction to the group (I) (Kiesler & Corbin, 1965; Kiesler, Zanna & deSalvo, 1966; Kiesler, 1969, 1971). Asch's (1955) experiments on individuals judging lengths of lines in a group context and Milgram's (1963) experiments in which a person in authority urges one subject to give electric shocks to another also illustrate the cybernetic hierarchy, with the effect of an individual's values (L) being the most important compared with I, G, or A variables.

FURTHER CONSIDERATIONS

In comparisons of the productivity of large groups with small groups, authoritarian leadership with democratic, centralized communication networks with decentralized, and cooperation with competition, the results are similar. For large groups, authoritarian leadership, centralized communication networks, or groups in which members are in competition, one finds an increase in productivity coupled with low satisfaction for the average member. An increase in group size, for example, reduces commitment (L), provides more skills and resources (A), requires more role differentiation while solidarity is harder to maintain (I), and requires more control on the part of the leadership.

One way to preserve the commitment and solidarity of the small group in a large group that has more resources, without using a form of centralized controlling leadership, is to use the method of consensus rather than majority vote or some other method of averaging individual opinions. Guidelines for the use of consensus, presented in the order L-A-I-G-L (see Chapter 4, Figure 4.1), have the effect of combining the best insights from all group members in a solution that incorporates all points of view or is accepted by the members as the best solution for the group at that time.

9
Dramaturgical Analysis:
Intergroup Relations in Israel

In an earlier period groups of Jews spent forty years in an exodus from Egypt, where they were slaves, to the land of Israel, where they were to act as a free people. It is written that forty years, or two generations, was prescribed for the exercise because it would take that long for the older generation to pass on, for them to shake off the slave mentality, and for a new consciousness to develop. The sojourn in the desert served as an "outward bound" experience, to toughen them up, and teach survival skills. In the Middle East the desert nomads have always been able to conquer more sedentary groups. Compared with the present day Israelis, who also have had forty years to develop a new consciousness, the earlier Israelites had several advantages. There were only twelve tribes to bring together, not an ingathering of many different peoples from many parts of the world. In those early days, there was also direct intervention from Heaven, so that it was clear which side was favored in the "holy war."

Only a limited number of options were suggested for dealing with the people who already occupied the land that the Israelites wished to take over. Members of any tribe already settled in the promised land were either to be killed or driven out. The idea that the land of Israel might include a sizable minority of Arabs and that in addition the Israelites should attempt to control territories with a population of more than one-and-a-half million Arabs was not envisioned.

For our consideration of problems of intergroup relations in present-day Israel, we begin by noting the population statistics that reveal the proportions of the various ethnic and other groups and the extent of conflict

This paper was originally presented at the Conference of the International Organization for the Study of Group Tensions, Princeton University, June 1988. Reprinted from *International Journal of Group Tensions*, 19, no. 2 (1989): 117-36.

between various groups over the past few years. Next we develop a form of dramaturgical analysis that can be used to provide a context for the examination of incidents of intergroup conflict, with special emphasis on the images that members of different groups have of themselves and each other. As examples of this type of analysis we describe an incident of "poisoning" on the West Bank, a Bedouin blood feud, and activities during the 1987-88 period of "unrest" in the occupied territories.

ISRAEL: A DIVIDED POPULATION

According to estimates of Benvenisti (*Jerusalem Post*, 18 March 1988), there are 1.09 million Palestinians in the West Bank and 650,000 in Gaza. The combined area of Israel and the territories thus contains about 60 percent Jews and 40 percent Arabs. However, the Arab birth rate is higher than that of the Jews so that the numbers in the two groups may be about equal by the year 2000. In addition to this major division of the population, there are further divisions within the Arab population based on religion and cultural background. On the Jewish side, the majority of the population come from North African and Asian traditions, and within each tradition groups are distinguished by degree of religious observance. Although equality for women in all areas of life has not been a tradition for either Jews or Arabs, the issue of women's rights is now in evidence. Within the Jewish population, with so many recent immigrants, prior nationality plays an important part in one's identity, especially as it divides the population into groups on the basis of home language.

Whereas other countries may have geographical boundaries that have been clearly defined for a long period of time, and thus it is clear if conflict occurs inside or outside of the country, this is not true for Israel. The boundaries of the country have been in question since the idea of a Jewish homeland was first put forward. Over the course of several wars, including the time when independence was acknowledged, the territory administered by Israel has continually expanded and contracted. The Sinai desert was a major instance of acquisition and evacuation. The West Bank and Gaza are contested areas. The smaller areas of East Jerusalem and the Golan Heights still present special problems, as does the security zone in Lebanon.

These areas should present enough problems of intergroup relations, however, as the United Jewish Appeal puts it, the Jews around the world are "One people, one destiny." Thus anything that happens to a Jew anywhere in the world can become a concern of Israelis. This also applies to any period of history, as is evident in the ongoing process of bringing perpetrators of the Holocaust to justice.

The idea that a conflict with Jews anywhere in the world is also an attack on Israel is unfortunately shared by some individuals and organizations. The activity of the Palestine Liberation Organization, with headquarters in

Tunisia, is an outstanding example of this phenomena. In addition, an incident between members of two different groups in Israel, that might pass unnoticed in any other part of the world, can quickly become a national and an international incident. For example, an Arab stabs a Jew in the market in Gaza. This leads to confrontations between Jews in a nearby town in Israel over the dedication of a monument to a former Arab notable, discussions in the Israeli parliament, statements by foreign governments, and resolutions in the United Nations (*Jerusalem Post*, 28 September through October 1986).

The other countries most frequently involved in some way with intergroup affairs in Israel either because of their proximity, their history, their attitude toward Jewish emigration, or their special relationship are: Egypt, Jordan, Syria, Lebanon, Germany, Russia, the United States, and South Africa. Although the conflict between Israel and the Arabs of the occupied territories and surrounding States was the dominant theme in 1988, Israel's President Herzog had observed a few years earlier, with a reference to Israel and in keeping with the tendency for "soul searching" that is characteristic of his culture: "The real enemy is within us" (*Jerusalem Post*, 20 June 1986). He was referring to conflicts between Israeli Jews and Israeli Arabs, and within the Jewish sector, between religious and secular, right and left, and Sephardim and Askenazim. A comprehensive analysis of intergroup relations in Israel would include examples of all these conflicts, such as disagreements over Sabbath movies, "Who is a Jew," the right of women to join religious councils, or benefits for development towns versus benefits for settlements in the occupied territories.

DRAMATURGICAL ANALYSIS

Dramaturgical analysis of social interaction assumes that a theatrical production is a model of the way life really is (Hare, Blumberg, et al., 1988). As a brief introduction to this approach, the five phases in the development of a social drama will be described, followed by a listing of the major variables in social interaction. Some of these variables are then applied in the analysis of types of dramatic situations, which in turn highlight some of the problems and solutions concerning intergroup relations in Israel.

PHASES IN THE DEVELOPMENT OF A SOCIAL DRAMA

Social dramas pass through five phases. First someone or some group defines a situation. This involves the presentation of an "actable idea" that may take the form of a compact *image* that is usually an emotionally loaded word picture, a *theme* with a direction of movement and an emotional tone, a *plot* with an indication of the major characters and the development of their relationship in a series of acts, or a *script* with detailed descriptions of the parts to be played. An example of an image that often appears in Bedouin blood feuds and in confrontations between Arabs and Jews is a gesture or verbal expression to indicate that the person presenting the image intends to dominate the person being confronted in the same way that a male may dominate a female during a sexual act. An example of a theme is the idea used by some Jewish settlers in the occupied territories that they will take a "Sabbath walk." The purpose of the walk is to demonstrate that they are free to wander anywhere in the territories, preferably close to an Arab village, however the walk could be in any direction as long as the mood is maintained. A plot is more complex since there is a clear indication of the major roles to be played and a series of events to be carried out. The street confrontations between Arab youth and Israeli soldiers have this character. The sequence of blocking a road, burning tires, throwing stones by the Arab youth, and shooting tear gas and rubber bullets and eventually dispersal by the soldiers using live ammunition is repeated over and over again. Scripted actions are seen in terrorist attacks across the borders into Israel, where the terrorists have been carefully schooled in the use of hang gliders or other equipment, and sometimes even carry written notes to remind them who they should hold hostage, what demands they should make, and which countries' ambassadors should be involved in the negotiations. In instances of intergroup relations there may be several dramas being enacted at the same time, some within the groups, some between the groups, with different degrees of explication of the "actable idea." In any case it is helpful to understand the degree to which the actors are being guided by an image, theme, plot, or script, to be able to predict the course of events.

The second phase involves locating or constructing an "action area," a stage or setting, together with the resources, props, costumes, and whatnot necessary for the performance. The action area may have a provision for an audience, both directly, in front of or around the area, and indirectly, through television, radio, or newspapers. There also may be backstage and offstage areas where persons prepare for action or carry out supporting activities. Kenneth Burke (1968) has called attention to the importance of the setting in his concept of the "scene/act" ratio. He suggests that there is a definite relationship between the scene and the action that will be carried out, in that the scene indicates the limits of appropriate action in that place. In a theater production when the curtain rises, the stage setting implies ambiguously, in time, place, and mood, the type of action that will be made explicit in the course of the drama. Thus it becomes important for those who wish to predict and control intergroup behavior to understand the implications for action in the choice of each setting, or "territory."

The third phase involves the selection of actors and the rehearsal, if necessary, of their roles. In some cases, aspects of a role, such as throwing stones or calling names, have been learned since childhood, and are readily available as part of an actor's repertoire. A complete production involves many roles: protagonists, antagonists, auxiliaries, audience members, directors, producers, and playwrights. One person may play a single role, or many, and the same role may be shared by a number of persons. For successful intervention on occasions of intergroup conflict new "third-party" roles may need to be introduced that were not considered by the conflicting sides.

The fourth phase is the one in which the actors perform the actable idea in the action area. There may be only one act, or a series of acts with scenes within the acts. Just as in the theater, where the curtain may be lowered to denote the passing of time between acts, so in real life the acts that form the drama need not occur at the same time nor in the same place. In the case of Israel, some of the same themes and plots that were formulated at the time of the Exodus are still being played out today. More than that, since the state of Israel is only forty years old, some of the actors who played major parts in the formation of the state are still on stage today. Some are still playing out ideas that were more appropriate at the time of independence and some, with a newer consciousness, searching for themes, plots, or scripts that would be more appropriate to today's realities. There is a sense in which Israel has no history, only current events, since images from the time of Exodus, through the Holocaust, and on to the present are continually being fused and reevaluated as a basis for action.

The last phase brings us full circle to the beginning, with a new definition of the situation. The fact that some action has taken place can provide new meanings for the actors, about themselves and about their abilities to cope with the situation, and for members of the audience who were not directly involved. Over the centuries, Jews have been a closely watched people and the themes that their actions appeared to represent have been evaluated, often to their detriment. It may be too soon in the course of history to expect a major national or international drama to be enacted without including a part for at least one Jew.

MAJOR VARIABLES IN SOCIAL INTERACTION

Social psychologists, whether studying behavior, attitudes, personality, or values, have frequently identified some or all of seven major variables in social interaction. Peabody and Goldberg (1989), after reviewing their own and others' research on personality, list the seven variables as follows:

1. Surgency: Bold-timid

2. Agreeableness: Warm-cold

3. Conscientiousness: Thorough-careless

4. Values: Moral-immoral

5. Emotional stability: Relaxed-tense

6. Culture: Intelligent-unintelligent

7. Evaluation: Good-bad

The example of each trait consists of two adjectives representing ends of a continuum. Each set has a high factor loading on the trait named and is representative of a number of bipolar sets that can be used to measure each variable.

The first four variables (surgency, agreeableness, conscientiousness, and values) represent independent dimensions that can be used to characterize types of behavior, attitudes, personality, or values. I consider the fifth variable (emotional stability) as an overall measure of variance. If needed, one could derive a measure of variance for each of the first four variables. The sixth variable of intelligence is usually measured by an I.Q. test, which in turn may consist of subscores for different skills such as verbal or mathematical ability. The seventh variable, of evaluation, is theoretically independent of the other six. No matter what combination of traits an individual or a group may have, it is quite possible that some individuals or groups will evaluate the constellation as "good," while others will evaluate the same constellation as "bad." For example, in Israel a person from one ethnic group or degree of religious observance throwing stones at another from a different group may be judged to be bold, cold, thorough, and moral (according to his or her own lights) by members of both groups. Yet one side may evaluate the behavior as "good" and the other side as "bad." However within some groups the evaluative variable may be highly correlated with one of the first four dimensions, especially with agreeableness, since persons who are warm often are thought to be "good" and persons who are "cold" often are thought to be "bad."

For the present analysis of intergroup relations, a similar list of variables is used, as follows:

1. Upward-Downward (Dominant-Submissive, indicated by being active or passive)
2. Positive-Negative (friendly or unfriendly)
3. Serious-Expressive (involved in the task or joking; note that the term "expressive" is used here with a different meaning than that given by Taylor for the first level of creativity in Figure 4.2)
4. Conforming-Anticonforming (guided by group norms or resisting pressure to conform)
5. Variance (within and between ratings)
6. Creativity (five levels, see Figure 4.2, Chapter 4)
7. Pro-Con (evaluated as good or bad)

Bales's SYMLOG theory contains six of the seven variables (Bales & Cohen, 1979; Hare, 1989a). Bales provides questionnaires that measure the dimensions Upward-Downward, Positive-Negative, and Forward-Backward (a combination of Variables 3 and 4, where Forward is serious and conforming and Backward is expressive and anticonforming). The questionnaires permit measures of variance both within sets of ratings for the same dimension and between sets of ratings. The evaluation of images, expressed in terms of the three SYMLOG dimensions, as to whether the person expressing the image is either in favor (Pro) or not in favor (Con) is a key element in the SYMLOG analysis. Since the two aspects of Bales's Forward-Backward dimension can be measured separately, using sets of Bales's own items (Hare, 1986b), the SYMLOG system provides measures of all but one of the seven major variables. The remaining variable of intelligence can be measured by any one of a number of existing intelligence tests, although for the present analysis, creativity is the aspect of intelligence that is emphasized.

For the comparison of summary measures of images of individuals, groups, and ideas, Bales's method of field diagrams is used. As an indication of the flow of creative activity by individuals and groups over time, figures are presented that plot levels of creativity against time, including the divisions of a social drama into acts and scenes.

POLTI'S DRAMATIC SITUATIONS

Polti, who was living in France in the early 1900s, sought to test the assertion of a drama critic that there were only a total of thirty-six dramatic situations that were repeated in various combinations in plays and stories (Polti, 1977). He collected some 1,000 stage plays and 200 other dramatic stories and sorted the dramatic situations into categories. At the conclusion of his work, Polti decided that there were only thirty-six situations after all, although he recognized that there were variations in the relationship between the characters, the extent of their free will, the amount of energy involved, and the extent of role differentiation.

The characters and the relationships between them in Polti's descriptions of the thirty-six dramatic situations were depicted in field diagrams (Hare, 1985b:167-170). The field diagrams were then sorted into sets according to system level and the interaction dimension that seemed to be dominant. For the present analysis we will focus on six types. Three are at the social system level, where the focus is on the interplay of several roles. Three are at the individual or personality level, where the conflict is between an individual and some overpowering force or on a conflict between different parts of the self. In each case the same three dimensions are involved: Upward-Downward, Positive-Negative, and Conforming-Anticonforming. Examples of each type at each system level are as follows:

Social System Level

1. U-D: A conflict between persons or groups of unequal power, or a struggle with some natural disaster.

2. P-N: A hero versus a villain, or a love/hate triangle.

3. C-A: Crime and punishment.

Individual or Personality Level

1. U-D: A search for someone or something by a powerless person.

2. P-N: A struggle between the positive and negative sides of the self (e.g., Dr. Jekyll and Mr. Hyde).

3. C-A: A conflict between conformity to an ideal versus some pragmatic action.

Since there appear to be a limited number of basic situations in interpersonal or intergroup activity, one can begin to develop methods of identifying these situations and strategies for dealing with the less desirable aspects of the conflicts involved. However the dimension of Serious-Expressive is missing from the list of dramatic situations. Polti had observed that any of the dramatic situations could be enacted in a serious or expressive (comic) vein. Thus to locate the missing dimension, we turn next to the four major types of dramatic productions that have been traditionally identified in the theater.

FOUR TYPES OF DRAMA

The four traditional types of drama can be classified in terms of "attribution theory" according to whether the outcome is judged to be good or bad and whether the cause is either some person (the self or another) or the situation (Hare, Blumberg, et al., 1988:16).

1. *Tragedy* has a bad outcome that is attributed to some person or persons.

2. *Comedy* has a good outcome, also attributed to a person or persons.

3. *Melodrama* has a bad outcome that is attributed to the situation in which the actors find themselves.

4. *Farce* has a good outcome, also dominated by the situation.

Tragedy and comedy are "character driven" in that they depend on the style of the principal characters or groups. Melodrama and farce are "plot driven" in that they depend on roles that can be played by almost anyone. In Israel, events in which Arik Sharon plays a central part can be seen as "character driven" since they tend to reflect a personal style that has been consistent since the days of the struggle for independence. On the other hand, the stone-throwing episodes in the occupied territories are "plot driven" since as quickly as one set of stone throwers is placed in a detention camp, another set comes forward to take their places. If a social drama is character driven, one must pay attention to the particular individuals involved. The drama is essentially a "psychodrama" (Moreno, 1953) where the action revolves around the personalities of the central protagonists. If the drama is plot driven, then the roles are the more important variables and the action is a "sociodrama." As noted above, to change these dramas, new "third-party" roles may need to be introduced to mediate between the conflicting groups.

Tragedy and melodrama are serious and comedy and farce expressive, although even the most serious dramas may have moments of expressive behavior for tension release. Also the most hilarious comic routine may provide for a period of less intense humor, such as a song, to give the audience some relief from their convulsive laughter. However the overall serious or expressive mood of the drama provides the "frame" (Goffman, 1974) for the whole activity. The other three dimensions of Upward-Downward, Positive-Negative, and Conforming-Anticonforming, indicate the nature of the dramatic situations within the drama.

THREE INTERGROUP EVENTS

Three intergroup events will be described briefly as examples of the application of a dramaturgical perspective for the analysis of intergroup relations. The first example involved many individuals and groups, although the activity that triggered the event was not what it appeared to be. This was a case of so-called "poisoning" of Arab schoolgirls on the West Bank in 1983. The second event, a Bedouin blood feud that continued over a twenty-year period, is an example of a type of event that has occurred many times in the past among traditional Bedouin tribesmen. The third event is the *intifada* (uprising) in the occupied territories that began in December 1987. In the course of each of these encounters, many images of persons and groups are used to justify actions or to motivate people to take sides in the conflict.

Poisoning on the West Bank

The account of "poisoning" on the West Bank in 1983 is based on newspaper articles in the *Jerusalem Post* (March and April). Other than a description of the school classroom where the first action took place and of a street that was the scene of a later action, there were no descriptions of the action areas (stages). The first step in the collection of the data was to construct a day-by-day description of activity. Some information comes from newspaper stories on the day after an incident and some is only revealed later at trials of participants or in reconstructions of actions through interviews. Two forms of summary figures are used in the analysis: a time line indicating the extent to which different individuals and groups seemed to be controlling the definition of the situation (Figure 9.1) and a field diagram indicating the location of the images of some of the participants from the Arab view and the Israeli view (Figure 9.2).

Figure 9.1
Levels of Creativity for Groups and Individuals Involved in Poisonings on the West Bank

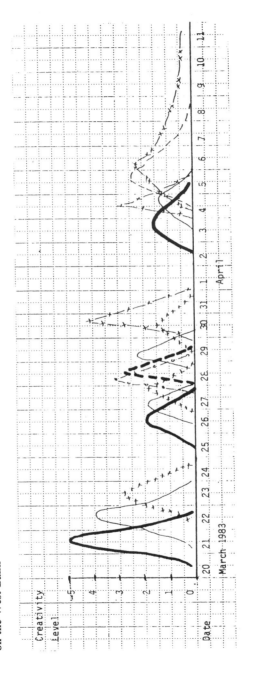

Key

━━ Arab schoolgirls
●–●● Arab villagers
── West Bank doctors
×××× Israeli Medical Unit
–·– Arab agitators

–·– Israeli Director General of Health
–××– Israeli military
---- Birzeit University Arab students

Figure 9.2
Images of Some of the Participants in Poisonings on the West Bank
from the Arab and Israeli Views

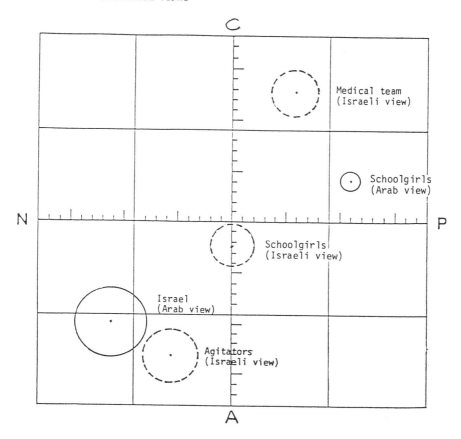

In the field diagram, the Positive-Negative dimension is the horizontal axis and the Conforming-Anticonforming dimension is the vertical axis. The Dominant-Submissive dimension is represented by the size of the circle surrounding the dot that locates the image on the P-N/C-A plane. The larger circles represent the dominant images and the smaller circles represent the submissive images.

Summary of the Event: On Monday, 21 March 1983, an Arab schoolgirl in Arrabe is not feeling well (presumably she is having a menstrual period). She goes to the window of the classroom to open the window for fresh air. She finds yellow dust on the window sill (presumably pollen) and notes an irritating odor (probably a cesspool). She concludes that she is being poisoned and a number of her schoolgirl classmates join her in reporting the same feelings. Next, West Bank doctors examine the girls and report severe symptoms. A day later an Israeli health team examines the area and finds no trace of a problem.

This sequence is repeated twice with different schoolgirls involved (March 26 and April 3). By the third time, provocateurs are on the scene as young men are found to be urging girls to say that they are being poisoned. In a fourth incident (March 28) Arabs living on one street report symptoms after a van with a broken exhaust pipe passes through. The Director General of Health for Israel defines the situation as mass hysteria. After the last incident, the Israeli military transfers students from West Bank hospitals to Israeli hospitals and detains agitators. The Director General again asserts that this is a mass phenomenon.

In addition to the activity of local groups, the International Red Cross is asked to give an opinion, a team of doctors from the United States is called in, World Health Organization doctors become involved, there is an appeal to the United Nations to investigate the incident, and Birzeit University Arab students hold a hunger strike to protest "poison annihilation of Palestinian people."

The use of the time line and the graphic representation of the levels of creativity of the various individuals and groups makes it possible to summarize visually the variation in the control of the "definition of the situation." We note that once a *plot* was established, with sequence of events and roles for the main participants, it could be enacted again and again by the same or different participants. Eventually, the Israeli military was used to remove the actors to another stage (hospital).

The field diagram (Figure 9.2) illustrates the different perceptions held by Arabs and Israelis of some of the major players in the drama. In the Arab view the innocent schoolgirls (Downward, Positive, and Conforming) were being poisoned by a hostile Israeli government that was acting beyond the limits of human decency (Upward, Negative, and Anticonforming). In the Israeli view the schoolgirls were at best hysterical and probably putting on a devious act (Upward and Anticonforming) at the urging of agitators (Upward, Negative, and Anticonforming). The interests of Israel were being represented by their medical team that was doing its job (Conforming). In this case members of each side held quite different images of the behavior of the main participants and acted in accordance with these images. In other cases, there may be agreement on the behavior or values, but disagreement as to the evaluation of the image as good or bad. The result is the same. Each side uses good images to indicate the desired behavior with members of the "ingroup" and negative images to justify conflict with the "outgroup."

Bedouin Blood Feud

Kressel (1982) provides an account of a blood feud between two Bedouin lineages in an urban settlement that lasted over a period of twenty years. This included ten years from the inception of the feud, through the main settlement in the mid-1960s, through the following ten-year period of adjustment to the new definition of the situation. In terms of Polti's dramatic situations, the blood feud is a conflict of power (dominance and submission), during which a lineage with a lower status in the community seeks to exchange positions with the lineage immediately above it in the status hierarchy.

The Bedouin lineage is graded hierarchically by its number of combatant male agnates, that is, men who are related through their fathers. Maternal kin are not considered blood relatives. Even in a war, women and children are not ordinarily considered as combatants unless they are in uniform. In this case, the initially lower status lineage brought in related families from Gaza to camp in nearby olive groves to increase the number of combatant males at the high point of the feud.

The feuds are conducted with definite rules. Even though a verbal threat is equated with a threat with a gun, traditionally guns are not used unless there is an escalation of the conflict. Weapons are limited to sticks and swords, although knives may be substituted for swords. An action area is selected so that an audience is always present to witness the violence, to assess the winners and losers, and to help bring about a settlement. However, an attack by members of one lineage on another usually is scheduled at night in a relatively secluded spot, often in a nearby olive grove. Thus an element of surprise is increased, darkness camouflages the reserve forces that may be on hand, and only a limited number of witnesses will be present. Later police will have a harder time gathering evidence and both winners and losers of the conflict can make exaggerated claims without being contradicted by third parties.

As noted in the description of an image, above, the main insults, by word or gesture, are sexual. They imply that the person making the insult has the power to assume the male role and dominate (rape) the other person who must assume the female role. These same traditional words and gestures appear in the televised record of the Arab uprising in the occupied territories in 1988, where the power struggle is now between the lower status Arabs and the higher status Jews.

In the Bedouin case, after ten years of conflict of varying degrees of intensity, and many attempts to control the violence by the local chief of police who well understood the Bedouin pattern of blood feuds, a traditional settlement was reached. Senior men from each side, together with third parties, met in a tent to decide what compensation should be made for any injuries to persons or damage to property that had occurred and to recognize the change in the status hierarchy.

Uprising in the Occupied Territories

Over the months of the uprising that began in December 1987 in the territories occupied by Israel there have been many incidents. The uprising began with the Arab response to a rumor that a car accident that claimed the lives of four Gaza men was a purposeful act on the part of the Israeli Jew who was driving the other vehicle. Each day stones are thrown by protesting Arab youth and Israeli police or army troops attempt to disperse the crowd with rubber bullets, water cannon, tear gas, and live ammunition. Some people are killed, more are wounded, and even more are detained. Although the massive Israeli forces that are used against the demonstrators may be able to contain or suppress an incident, the pattern of interaction, when the uprising erupts again, is essentially the same.

What can be done to change the pattern? Following the dramaturgical perspective, one can intervene to change the pattern at each of the five phases of a dramatic production. Interventions in early phases of a drama can be expected to be more effective than interventions in later phases. In the first phase one can introduce a new actable idea or modify the existing image, theme, plot, or script so that the resulting drama involves cooperation rather than competition and conflict. In the second phase one can choose or control the action area to avoid direct confrontation or to enhance cooperation. In the third phase one can provide variations in the roles that the actors are accustomed to playing, for example by rehearsing nonviolent methods of confrontation to replace their violent methods or by adding new third-party roles, often played by actors who are not committed to either of the sides in the dispute. Once the action has begun, in the fourth phase, third parties and others can intervene directly, by placing themselves between the conflicting sides or by dealing with provocateurs or other especially volatile members of the crowd. In the final phase, of new meanings, it may still be possible to show, if it is true, that for various reasons the instance of conflict that has just occurred need not set a pattern for future encounters. Demonstrations of reconciliation can be arranged to secure commitment to future acts of cooperation.

The most extensive experience with interventions in protests and intercommunal riots is available in India, especially in the activities of the Gandhian Peace Brigade (Shanti Sena). Narayan Desai, one of the leaders of the present-day Gandhian movement in India, has recorded several examples of interventions in communal riots between Muslims and Hindus (Desai, 1972:21-48). When a riot breaks out in an Indian town, the Peace Brigade members, who are ordinarily doing community development work in other towns or villages in the area, are called together. In a typical example, about thirty members of the Peace Brigade form three sets to play different roles. Two of the senior members become the negotiating team to visit officials in the town and eventually to bring leaders of the Muslim and Hindu communities together to arrange a reconciliation. A second small group of four persons has the responsibility for checking rumors and providing accurate facts so that individuals or crowds will not rush into action on the basis of false or exaggerated information. If the riot goes on over a period of weeks or months, this team may produce a newsletter to give accurate information and to provide accounts of effective nonviolent encounters or interventions. The third set of Peace Brigade members are divided into teams of five or six persons to go into the streets, placing themselves between conflicting groups if necessary, providing first aid, cleaning the streets, and carrying out other health or sanitation services that may have been disrupted because people are afraid to move about on the streets.

Although it is doubtful that very many people in Israel have ever heard of the Gandhian Peace Brigade, the daily press carries accounts of instances where some persons have intervened in a similar manner, or more often, where this type of intervention would have been especially relevant. One example would be concerned with rumor control, which has to do with the first phase of a drama by introducing an actable idea. During the uprising a group of American academics attended a conference on the West Bank (*Jerusalem Post*, 29 March 1988). At the end of the conference a bus trip was arranged to a nearby Arab village. On the way to the village the bus driver explained their activity to the soldiers at a checkpoint near the village. The visitors were well received by the villagers. Unfortunately, while their visit was in progress, a person from a nearby Jewish settlement reported that a busload of visitors had been hijacked. On the strength of this unconfirmed report, troops were rushed to the village, a violent confrontation ensued, and an Arab boy was killed.

On the positive side, on some occasions the police or military have prevented demonstrators from gaining access to a religious site or some other area that would have special connotations should a conflict occur there. Various groups have held nonviolent marches, vigils, fasts, or other actions to show that a point of view can be stated without violence. Other groups have held conferences, workshops, or other forms of discussions that include both Arabs and Jews, to demonstrate that dialogue is possible and to provide individuals with personal experience with members of a different background. On one occasion a peace group of Jews and Arabs, who were patrolling an area where demonstrations were expected, arrived at a village on the border of the West Bank as Border Police were firing tear gas at Arab villagers. The peace activists positioned themselves between the Border Police and the stone-throwing villagers, then negotiated with the villagers to disperse (*Jerusalem Post*, 31 March 1988).

CONCLUSION

Thus, as with any other social-psychological theory that identifies different categories of interaction, the dramaturgical perspective can be used to sort instances of intergroup relations into types. One can then note the distribution of types, the structures and processes associated with each type, and the outcomes of different combinations of structure and process. One may then find that older forms of intervention in intergroup conflicts, such as the experience of the Gandhian Peace Brigade, can be understood in a new light, and further that new forms of intervention may suggest themselves. In every case, as in Israel, it is important to understand the cultural background of the members of the various groups, to be aware of their traditional symbols and to be clear about the part played by these images in the basic identities of the groups. For as Iago observed to Othello: "Who steals my purse steals trash; . . . but he who filches from me my good name . . . makes me poor indeed" (Shakespeare, *Othello*, Act 3, Scene 3). This applies to all parties in the conflict.

10
Exchange Analysis

Exchange theory is based in the idea that social interaction is similar to economic behavior in that it involves an exchange of material and nonmaterial goods and services. Persons enter into new relationships or continue with old ones as long as there is some profit as a result of the transaction.

Within the social-psychological literature, the major contributions to exchange theory have been made by Thibaut and Kelley (1959, 1986), who used a "payoff matrix" approach; Homans (1974), who focused on informal groups; and Blau (1964), who was interested in exchanges within organizational settings. Gergen, Greenberg, and Willis (1980) have edited a comprehensive examination of theories of social exchange. Some recent work on exchange is concerned with exchanges within a single category of behavior, such as power, or with the criterion for an effective exchange, such as equity or justice (Cook, 1987). For example, Foddy (1989) discusses information control as a bargaining tactic, and Hatfield (1983) provides an overview of research on equity theory. Turner (1989) combines exchange theory with a dramaturgical perspective. (See also Blumberg, 1992.)

Both Blau (1964) and Foa and Foa (1974, 1980) have provided lists of the major categories of "goods and services" that are involved in social exchange, although they have not used them for systematic act-by-act analysis. Blau identifies six types of rewards that he classifies as either intrinsic, extrinsic, or unilateral and again as either spontaneous evaluations or calculated actions. An example of an intrinsic reward that is spontaneous is personal attraction and a calculated reward is social acceptance. Similarly extrinsic rewards include social approval and instrumental services and unilateral rewards include respect and compliance.

Foa and Foa arrange their list of resources in a circumplex:

Money

Information   Goods

Status   Services

Love

They suggest that the display represents two main dimensions: from abstract and intangible (on the left) to concrete and tangible (on the right); from universalistic (at the top) to particularistic (at the bottom).

Although Bales's (1950) categories for Interaction Process Analysis were developed before exchange theory became popular, they can be used to analyze social exchange with regard to the contributions that individuals make to the problem-solving process. With their original definitions, the twelve IPA categories are as follows (Bales, 1950:9):

1. *Shows solidarity*, raises other's status, gives help, reward.
2. *Shows tension release*, jokes, laughs, shows satisfaction.
3. *Agrees*, shows passive acceptance, understands, concurs, complies.
4. *Gives suggestion*, direction, implying autonomy for the other.
5. *Gives opinion*, evaluation, analysis, expresses feeling, wish.
6. *Gives orientation*, information, repeats, clarifies, confirms.
7. *Asks for orientation*, information, repetition, confirmation.
8. *Asks for opinion*, evaluation, analysis, expression of feeling.
9. *Asks for suggestion*, direction, possible ways of action.
10. *Disagrees*, shows passive rejection, formality, withholds help.
11. *Shows tension*, asks for help, withdraws out of field.
12. *Shows antagonism*, deflates other's status, defends or asserts self.

Six of the categories (1, 2, 3, 10, 11, 12) describe social-emotional behavior and six of the categories (4, 5, 6, 7, 8, 9) describe task behavior. Within the task categories, three types of processes are recorded: orientation, opinion, and suggestion. These three types are coded directly according to two modalities of exchange: gives and asks for. Since Bales recorded his categories on a moving paper tape or with some other device that preserved the order in which remarks were made, it was also possible to identify which of the task categories was followed by either agreement or disagreement. Three modalities that are identified separately in other category systems (to be noted below) are included in Bales's "disagree" category. These are "reject," "deprive," and "ignore." Bales's Category 3, "agrees," which included acceptance, is coded as "accepts" in other systems, placing more emphasis on the exchange. Since all three modalities of disagreement rarely account for more than 10 percent of the interaction in problem-solving groups (Bales &

Hare, 1965), the lack of a finer discrimination of categories probably will have little effect on the analysis for this type of group. However the IPA categories still only record the *process* of interaction. Other schemes must be added if the *content* of the interaction is important.

Morley and Stephenson (1977) developed a comprehensive category system for the analysis of bargaining in labor-management negotiations. They include nine categories for content as a "resource." A brief description of their system is given in Chapter 12. In that chapter, I introduce a category system that codes content in terms of levels of creativity and process in terms of dimensions of interpersonal behavior. The remainder of this chapter describes Longabaugh's system and the version I developed with John Mueller. Both schemes describe content in terms of functional (AGIL) categories. In terms of the cybernetic hierarchy (see Chapter 8), the AGIL categories have a similar ranking to the levels of creativity, with "A" similar to creativity at Level 2 and "L" similar to creativity at Level 5. The AGIL version may be more useful if there is only a written record of transactions available for analysis.

LONGABAUGH'S EXCHANGE CATEGORIES

Although, as noted above, Blau described six categories that represent the basic set of rewards used in social exchange, he did not use these categories as a formal system for the analysis of act-by-act behavior in groups. Longabaugh (1963) proposed a set of categories and a method of analysis for exchange, but his system was designed for the observation of mother-child dyads and is not comprehensive enough for general use. However, it did provide a model for a system developed by Hare and Mueller (1979) that uses a set of categories based on Parsonian functional (AGIL) theory (see Chapter 8). The analysis of a part of a transcript of a group psychotherapy session, given at the end of this chapter, illustrates the use of the revised system.

Longabaugh saw two parts of exchange acts that could be coded: *resource salience*, the content, and *modality*, the way that the content is handled by the actors in exchange. Longabaugh divided salient resources into three classes: information, control (freedom and direction), and support. His six modalities were seeking, offering, depriving, accepting, ignoring, and rejecting. These three salient resources in six modalities provided eighteen categories plus a nineteenth, called "unscorable behavior." The nineteenth category included acts that were so incomplete as to be unclassifiable and residual acts that were not judged to constitute exchange.

The Longabaugh categories were specific to the requirements of observing and rating mother-child dyads, and Longabaugh commented on the limitations of his system for other purposes. He recognized, for example, that the ability to distinguish different kinds of information was important, and that support might have been divided into two classes of esteem and comfort. Splitting "support" into two types brings Longabaugh's categories more into line with the Parsonian categories:

Information:	subset of A;
Control:	subset of G;
Comfort:	subset of I;
Esteem:	subset of L.

Thus, while the Longabaugh and Hare-Mueller category systems are similar in their treatment of modality, the primary contribution of the revised category system is the employment of the AGIL concepts. The Parsonian categories are more exhaustive with regard to content, since the AGIL framework seems capable of subsuming all social behavior. The AGIL categories are also more specific in distinguishing content and more suitable for the task of analyzing group process.

The reliability of the Hare-Mueller category system should be very similar to Longabaugh's, since the same six modalities are used with a redefinition of the salient resources. Longabaugh (1963) used as a measure of reliability the percentage of act agreement (number of act agreements divided by the number of act agreements plus the number of act disagreements). Two observers were considered to agree on scoring a given act if they coded the same person as actor, the same modality for the act, and the same resource as salient in the act. Coding was done on the spot after training with written protocols. Longabaugh reported a median percentage of act agreement for forty-nine experimental sessions of 60 percent, with a range from 38 percent to 92 percent.

A REVISED NOTATION FOR EXCHANGE ANALYSIS

In applying abstract exchange theory in a line-by-line analysis of a group psychotherapy transcript, we are interested in the content of the exchange (in terms of A, G, I, or L), the bids and requested bids for the commodity to be exchanged, who is "buying" and who is "selling," and whether the exchange is actually completed.

We might view the group as a corporation interested in collectively buying commodities. The group leader, in this case the therapist, is the chairman of the board, and the amount of influence that he wields in decisions about buying these commodities depends on his style of leadership and the degree to which any subgroups endorse or oppose his authority. In a psychotherapy group, individual members are stockholders with a greater or lesser voting influence and also suppliers of the commodities such as information and feelings, that the group is seeking.

The exchanges are notationally represented in the following manner. The person who is initiating the action, a call for bids or a bid, is represented by the first capital letter in the notation. The next capital letter represents the person who is the object of the action. The next letter, in lower case, represents one of the six modalities used in exchanges:

s—seeks
o—offers
d—deprives
a—accepts
i—ignores
r—rejects

The last letter, a capital A,G,I, or L, indicates the functional description of the commodity (for example):

A—money, information
G—power, control
I—influence, comfort
L—commitment, esteem

Often the last letter has a subscript to differentiate between different commodities, since content is important in exchange analysis.

A few lines from the transcript can be used for illustration:

Larry (therapist):	What do you feel about this?
Bill (patient):	Nothing.
Larry:	Nothing at all?

Larry is asking Bill for information about his feelings. This is coded as L B sA_2. The symbol A_2 is used because the information is of a certain type, as we shall see when we examine the transcript. Bill replies with a bid of information, B L oA_2. Larry does not accept this bid, L B rA_2. If Larry had accepted Bill's reply as valid, it would have been noted as L B aA_2. The whole interchange looks like this:

L B sA_2
B L oA_2
L B rA_2

Although at least three lines are necessary for an exchange to occur, the negotiation often goes on much longer for a single exchange.

Transcript Analysis

As an illustration of the use of exchange analysis of a session of group psychotherapy with alcoholics, we include part of a transcript from a group at the William Slater Hospital in Cape Town. The first section of the complete transcript does not contain proceedings of the group proper. Patients are coming in the whole time, and the topic of conversation concerns who should be in the group, or in the AGIL categories, L_i, since it is a basic question of membership, L, concerning the relations between the group members, I. It is almost as if an admission ticket is required for group membership, a ticket which consists of being either Larry's or Joy's patient. It is apparent that some people don't have a ticket, but Larry is not the ticket collector; he's just asking whether all the patients are sure they have the correct tickets. The ticket collector, as it turns out, comes in later. Steve comes in to announce that Charles and Fred don't have tickets for this group, but do have them for the downstairs group, and the two patients leave.

Larry begins to define the type of behavior that is expected from the patients in the group, or, we might say, to define the exchange contract for the session. He says that he and Joy know the patients better than anyone else, so the patients should feel free to discuss personal problems, implying that the two therapists can offer sympathy and understanding (I) to the patients. Then Larry announces what commodities are and are not being sought for the group's collective buying. It turns out to be information (A). The unwanted information (denoted $A-$) is talking about drinking. What is being sought is A_1, information about problems leading up to and resulting from drinking; A_2, information about general feelings and concerns of the patient; and A_3, information about proposed solutions. The rewards to the patients which are to proceed from these solutions, and therefore presumably the criteria for judging the worth of the solutions, are getting well again, staying dry, and leading a satisfying life. By asking for this information, Larry has opened the floor for bidding.

In some cases, there is negotiation of the terms of this contract by the group, for we remember that it is the group as a whole that is buying these commodities, but in this group the contract put forward by the chairman of the board is accepted without comment, and George springs into action, perhaps a little prematurely, with a bid announcing that he has some A_1 to sell: information about the problems leading up to his drinking problem. In comes the ticket collector to interrupt the proceedings, but Willie resumes the proceedings by asking to know a little more about George's product (sA_1). Johann and Laurence signify their approval of the product (aA_1); they cast their votes to buy by elaborating on George's presentation (oA_1). In this they are showing solidarity with George, so we rate them as offering I to him (oI).

Laurence offers some A_3 to go along with George's A_1 (oA_3), but there is disagreement about this new contribution after George describes the proposed solution as "dutch courage" (oA_3), and Bill summarily dismisses the bid for A_3: "Forget about the dutch courage" (rA_3).

Finally Larry re-enters with a request for some information about George's original product A_1 (sA_1), his explanation that he drinks because he is shy. George doesn't appear to be able to elaborate much, and Willie comes in with his vote against buying George's product, saying that George doesn't show shyness in the group or in the hospital (rA_1): in effect, Willie offers George support or liking (oI) as a consolation for casting his vote against George's A_1.

This was not a final decision in the group, because the bartering for this single exchange goes on for quite a while after the point at which the transcript ends, but the group never did buy George's commodity.

In the middle section of the transcript Larry calls for $A+$ bids from third-week patients, and Willie and Bill announce that they are prepared to oblige. Larry concentrates on Bill and asks specifically for A_2 (information about feelings) and A_3 (information about proposed solutions). After an interlude of interchange for circumstantial information, Bill reveals his commodity, A_3 (a proposed solution): He is going to divorce his wife. But Larry is more interested in getting A_2: What are Bill's feelings about the decision? Bill replies with what we label A_{20}, the zero signifying that Bill claims he has no feelings about it. Larry does not accept this last commodity (rA_{20}), but Bill persists in offering it (oA_{20}), in effect ignoring the rejection [$i(rA_{20})$], but also offering his oversupplied commodities A_3 and $A-$ instead. Bill rejects Larry's A_{2E} (where "2E" is used to note the suggestion that Bill's emotions and his drinking problem are related) before it is even offered for the first time.

The negotiations fly for quite a while in this vein, with Larry seeking Bill's A_2 and offering A_{2E}, while Bill attempts to create a market for A_3, $A-$, and even a new commodity, A_{1A} (where "1A" is used to record the claim that he drank because he was simply fatigued).

Finally, Bill accepts Larry's proffered A_{2E}, but dealing continues as Larry perseveres in trying to secure some adequate A_2. When Bill signals that his only available A_2 commodity is A_{20}, Larry calls for help from Steve (L S $sI+$) and gets it (S L $oI+$).

Steve redraws the contract, offering to give $I+$, being able to "feel with (the patients)" (S P $oI+$) in exchange for $A+$, acceptable information (S P $sA+$). He reviews the negotiations (S B sA_2) and emphasizes that A_{20} is not good enough (S B rA_{20}), and suggests that Bill has a secret cache of A_2 (S B oA_2). What follows is an interesting negotiation concerning the relative values of the various commodities and has to do with the cybernetic hierarchy (see Chapter 8). Bill insists that his feelings, an L factor and therefore highest in the cybernetic hierarchy, are of less importance than the divorce, which is an I factor because it has to do with social role (L < I). Steve asserts the opposite (L > I). Bill, in return, compares his feelings toward his wife and son with damaged tools, an analogy that would place them at the bottom of the hierarchy as A factors, and reasserts the supreme importance of the divorce decision (L = A < I).

The following excerpt from the transcript beginning with Bill's acceptance of Larry's offer and ending with the discussion of "damaged tools" illustrates the exchange notation:

L B oA$_{2E}$	Larry:	But are you, are you sure that it's not related to something which you might feel makes you really upset—say, feelings of rejection, or people not liking you, or things like that?
B L aA$_{2E}$	Bill:	You're right, I do.
L B sA$_2$	Larry:	I mean, can you identify things that really upset you?
B L oA	Bill:	O yes, absoutely, absolutely, it's there. More so in the last two-and-a-half years since I've been living there. Because I bought the property from the post office—through the post office, not that it makes any difference—but the rule states that if you invest in a house, you as the buyer, the owner, must live in that house, so of course I was forced to go and live with my family again. But before I was living away. Before I came here I was living in hotels, and I got out of that because I was drinking too heavily. But uh, these last two-and-a-half years plus, I've, I've had to uh, live here, to get the
B L oA$_{2E}$		uh subsidy. And in that time I've had time to analyze the attitude in the house. Underground friction, uneasiness.
L B sA$_2$,	Larry:	Have you had time to analyze yourself?
B L dA$_2$	Bill:	Myself? Well, myself is according to my history as was stated
B L oA$_3$		in my uh autobiography. But uh, having done what I had done, I bought the property, mainly for my son. And the
B L aA$_2$		attitude in the house has been such by him and his mother, I thought it was so stupid, and of course uh, I'm not insensitive to these things: These things upset me.
L B oA$_2$	Larry:	That's what I'm saying: You know you, they're really rejecting you, by saying that—
B L aA$_2$	Bill:	Yes.
L B sA$_2$	Larry:	And how d'you react to rejection?
B L oA$_2$	Bill:	I keep quiet, just keep quiet. Because I know what's going to
B L oA$_3$		happen. They think I'm treating that wrongly. I've already spoken to them. The subject remains the same. So they've had their warning. But I didn't tell them that "there's going to be quite a change in this house." They don't answer. No
B L oA$_{20}$		temper, no nothing. I can't I can't, I have, I can't be bothered

		having a temperament, going into a temper for that, even when I was drinking. I couldn't be bothered. It's a waste of energy.
L S sI +	Larry:	I, I'm sure for instance Steve would, would disagree with you completely about that. Steve, what do you think?
S L oI +	Steve (nurse):	Yah, (Bill), you know, um, I've once thought, well at the
Contract:		beginning, you know, when somebody talks, and I can feel
S P sA +		with them, you know, and really live myself into the situa-
S P oI +		tion, and you seem to just on a superficial level, just pour out, and don't really give anything of yourself, you know,
S B sA$_2$		and um I, I do feel it is healthy to express your feelings and it's, it's, it's not good to keep it inside. And I think that that's what you're doing, you know, you're saying, "O,
S B rA$_{20}$		they're rejecting me," and, and you know, "I don't feel very
S B oA$_2$		much about it," and in reality I think you do feel a hell of a lot.
B S aA$_2$	Bill:	I do feel it. But I know how I am going to end it. And then
B S oA$_3$		I'll feel better [L < I.]
S B sA$_2$	Steve:	But can you share some of your feelings with us?
B S dA$_2$	Bill:	I don't think it's going to uh help in this sense, because I've made my decision, and after all to hear it.
S B sA$_2$	Steve:	I think so, I think it's going to help you quite a lot, because the feelings are still going to be there, you know, it's unre-solved, it's there. [L > I.]
S B rA$_3$		You must work with them, otherwise you know you're not going to stop it just by divorcing your wife.
	Bill:	I have one method of living: that if a tool is damaged, there's only one way for it—throw it away. It's of no use to me, or to my life. [L = A < I.]
B S oA$_3$		And if my marriage is damaged, and my relationship with my son is damaged—
S B sA$_2$	Steve:	How do you feel about that, (Bill), you know you—
B S oA$_2$	Bill:	That I don't like. That, that's going to last longer than any-thing else.
S B sA$_2$	Steve:	Hmm. What effects does it, has it got on you—how does it make you feel inside?
B S oA$_2$	Bill:	Well, I'm terribly disappointed, and uh it does work on me.
B S oA$_3$		But uh, that is something I just have to live with. I can't make anybody like me or love me if they don't want to.
S B sA$_3$	Steve:	Have you ever tried?

Steve perceptively pursues the angle of the son, which touches a nerve, and succeeds in getting Bill to express some real emotions about the relationship to his son. But Bill reverts for a while to offering more A_3. When he returns to the A_2 after a long monologue, Steve reinforces the behavior and clinches the exchange as outlined in his contract, giving $I+$ for A_2. At this point the therapy really begins, and Steve begins to explore with Bill the ramifications of his feelings toward wife and son. This runs into a snag when Bill refuses to disclose a particularly important fact about himself that he feels would be threatening to reveal. Steve appeals to the group at large without success to bring pressure on Bill, and then Larry steps back in and observes that individual facts are not as important as the expression of feelings, and says he does not want to damage the exchange so arduously set up for the sake of relatively unimportant information.

The exchange pattern proceeds, with Bill offering his A_2, and Steve supplying his $I+$ to fulfill his side of the bargain.

The "typical ending" of this psychotherapy group might be seen as an audit held after bidding and buying has been closed down, to determine what kind of profit the interested parties have secured. Larry refers back to the original contract, one of the clauses of which indicated that patients would gain the reward of feeling better in return for the cost of information, when he asks if Bill is feeling better. Bill indicates that he has turned a small profit, and Larry tries to reinforce the exchange by approving Bill's expression of feelings.

The whole analysis, likened to an auction in a corporation, may seem rather metaphorical. But the simile itself is more an illustrative terminology to aid in understanding the exchanges than a concept crucial to the category system or the theory of social exchange. Terms like "admission tickets," "bidding," "buying," "commodities," and "auditing," although heuristically adequate, could be exchanged for duller terminology, but this would increase the reader's cost in tedium, and probably terminate the exchange.

The Profit in Exchange Analysis for Group Therapists

Question: What are the uses of the category system for staff conducting therapy groups?

Answer: It is a systematic way of looking at social behavior, and can help explain why some therapeutic approaches are more successful than others.

Question: Why, for example, is Steve's approach in the transcript fairly successful?

Answer: Because he states explicitly for the patient what he is going to do. The contract calls for an exchange of information for support. When he receives information from the patient, he sees to it that he gives support. The behavior is reinforced and trust in the patient-therapist exchange relationship is built for the future. It is not expected that the staff member keep a running coding of the exchanges, but the system helps him or her to question whether or not the patient is receiving enough profit to continue with the therapy.

By noting the exchanges a person is willing to make, one becomes aware of the person's hierarchy of values, what seems to be potentially the most rewarding outcome, and what are acceptable costs. This in turn will indicate that person's willingness to take on a new role, such as that of the "good patient," or to give up an old one, such as that of "alcoholic." Since each role involves a set of rights and duties, it is important to be able to judge the extent to which an actor will accept the rewards and bear the costs.

11
SYMLOG Analysis

SYMLOG, an acronym for a SYstem for the Multiple Level Observation of Groups, was developed over a period of forty years by Bales and associates at Harvard University. After retirement from the university Bales continued to expand the theory through programs written for the SYMLOG Consulting Group to analyze behavior of management teams. Bales's major statement concerning the SYMLOG approach was published in 1979 (Bales & Cohen, 1979). More recently, a collection of research reports with the emphasis on the application of the theory (Polley, Hare & Stone, 1988) and a review of the research using SYMLOG through 1988 (Hare, 1989a) have been published.

Research prior to the development of SYMLOG had indicated that three bipolar characteristics of values and behavior are fundamental: (1) Dominance versus Submissiveness, (2) Friendliness versus Unfriendliness, and (3) Acceptance versus Nonacceptance of authority. The three dimensions can be visualized in the form of a cube (see Figure 11.1). The vertical dimension indicates Dominance (Upward) to Submissiveness (Downward). The horizontal dimension is Friendliness (Positive, on the right) to Unfriendliness (Negative, on the left). The third dimension goes from Acceptance of authority (Forward) to Nonacceptance of authority (Backward).

When each of these dimensions is divided into three, the result is a large cube containing twenty-seven smaller cubes, each representing one to three vectors. The small cube in the center of the large cube represents values or behavior that is "average," neither high nor low in any direction. To derive measures of each of the three dimensions, questionnaires or observation forms are used containing twenty-six statements, each representing the combination of vectors in one of the small cubes. An example of the value form is given in Figure 11.2 and the behavior form in Figure 11.3. The forms are designed to be machine coded.

Figure 11.1
The SYMLOG Cube Diagram

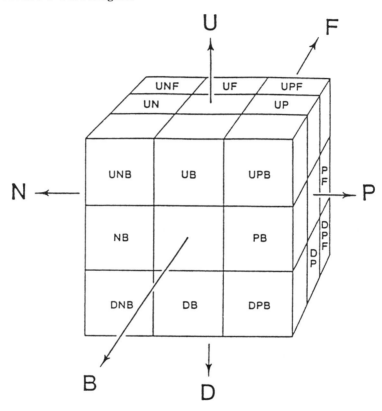

Source: From Robert F. Bales, "Overview of the SYMLOG System: Measuring and Changing Behavior in Groups," p. 11 (San Diego: SYMLOG Consulting Group, 1988). Reprinted by permission of SYMLOG Consulting Group.

Notes: Metaphorical names for the physical directions coordinated with names for describing the value directions for individual and organizational values:

U = "Upward" = Values on Dominance;
D = "Downward" = Values on Submissiveness;
P = "Positive" = Values on Friendliness;
N = "Negative" = Values on Unfriendliness;
F = "Forward" = Values on Acceptance of Authority;
B = "Backward" = Values on Nonacceptance of Authority

Figure 11.2
Individual and Organizational Values, Answer Sheet

ANSWER SHEET

QUESTION # ... ⊏1⊐ ⊏2⊐ ⊏3⊐ ⊏4⊐ ⊏5⊐ ⊏6⊐ ⊏7⊐ ⊏8⊐ ⊏9⊐   ⊏A⊐ ⊏B⊐ ⊏C⊐ ⊏D⊐ ⊏E⊐ ⊏F⊐ ⊏G⊐ ⊏H⊐

Rater's Code Name: (3 vertical letters)

RATER
⊏A⊐ ⊏B⊐ ⊏C⊐ ⊏D⊐ ⊏E⊐ ⊏F⊐ ⊏G⊐ ⊏H⊐ ⊏I⊐ ⊏J⊐ ⊏K⊐ ⊏L⊐ ⊏M⊐ ⊏N⊐ ⊏O⊐ ⊏P⊐ ⊏Q⊐ ⊏R⊐ ⊏S⊐ ⊏T⊐ ⊏U⊐ ⊏V⊐ ⊏W⊐ ⊏X⊐ ⊏Y⊐ ⊏Z⊐
⊏A⊐ ⊏B⊐ ⊏C⊐ ⊏D⊐ ⊏E⊐ ⊏F⊐ ⊏G⊐ ⊏H⊐ ⊏I⊐ ⊏J⊐ ⊏K⊐ ⊏L⊐ ⊏M⊐ ⊏N⊐ ⊏O⊐ ⊏P⊐ ⊏Q⊐ ⊏R⊐ ⊏S⊐ ⊏T⊐ ⊏U⊐ ⊏V⊐ ⊏W⊐ ⊏X⊐ ⊏Y⊐ ⊏Z⊐

Code Name of Persons or Concepts Rated: (3 vertical letter code names)

1
⊏A⊐ ⊏B⊐ ⊏C⊐ ⊏D⊐ ⊏E⊐ ⊏F⊐ ⊏G⊐ ⊏H⊐ ⊏I⊐ ⊏J⊐ ⊏K⊐ ⊏L⊐ ⊏M⊐ ⊏N⊐ ⊏O⊐ ⊏P⊐ ⊏Q⊐ ⊏R⊐ ⊏S⊐ ⊏T⊐ ⊏U⊐ ⊏V⊐ ⊏W⊐ ⊏X⊐ ⊏Y⊐ ⊏Z⊐
⊏A⊐ ⊏B⊐ ⊏C⊐ ⊏D⊐ ⊏E⊐ ⊏F⊐ ⊏G⊐ ⊏H⊐ ⊏I⊐ ⊏J⊐ ⊏K⊐ ⊏L⊐ ⊏M⊐ ⊏N⊐ ⊏O⊐ ⊏P⊐ ⊏Q⊐ ⊏R⊐ ⊏S⊐ ⊏T⊐ ⊏U⊐ ⊏V⊐ ⊏W⊐ ⊏X⊐ ⊏Y⊐ ⊏Z⊐
⊏A⊐ ⊏B⊐ ⊏C⊐ ⊏D⊐ ⊏E⊐ ⊏F⊐ ⊏G⊐ ⊏H⊐ ⊏I⊐ ⊏J⊐ ⊏K⊐ ⊏L⊐ ⊏M⊐ ⊏N⊐ ⊏O⊐ ⊏P⊐ ⊏Q⊐ ⊏R⊐ ⊏S⊐ ⊏T⊐ ⊏U⊐ ⊏V⊐ ⊏W⊐ ⊏X⊐ ⊏Y⊐ ⊏Z⊐

2
⊏A⊐ ⊏B⊐ ⊏C⊐ ⊏D⊐ ⊏E⊐ ⊏F⊐ ⊏G⊐ ⊏H⊐ ⊏I⊐ ⊏J⊐ ⊏K⊐ ⊏L⊐ ⊏M⊐ ⊏N⊐ ⊏O⊐ ⊏P⊐ ⊏Q⊐ ⊏R⊐ ⊏S⊐ ⊏T⊐ ⊏U⊐ ⊏V⊐ ⊏W⊐ ⊏X⊐ ⊏Y⊐ ⊏Z⊐
⊏A⊐ ⊏B⊐ ⊏C⊐ ⊏D⊐ ⊏E⊐ ⊏F⊐ ⊏G⊐ ⊏H⊐ ⊏I⊐ ⊏J⊐ ⊏K⊐ ⊏L⊐ ⊏M⊐ ⊏N⊐ ⊏O⊐ ⊏P⊐ ⊏Q⊐ ⊏R⊐ ⊏S⊐ ⊏T⊐ ⊏U⊐ ⊏V⊐ ⊏W⊐ ⊏X⊐ ⊏Y⊐ ⊏Z⊐
⊏A⊐ ⊏B⊐ ⊏C⊐ ⊏D⊐ ⊏E⊐ ⊏F⊐ ⊏G⊐ ⊏H⊐ ⊏I⊐ ⊏J⊐ ⊏K⊐ ⊏L⊐ ⊏M⊐ ⊏N⊐ ⊏O⊐ ⊏P⊐ ⊏Q⊐ ⊏R⊐ ⊏S⊐ ⊏T⊐ ⊏U⊐ ⊏V⊐ ⊏W⊐ ⊏X⊐ ⊏Y⊐ ⊏Z⊐

3
⊏A⊐ ⊏B⊐ ⊏C⊐ ⊏D⊐ ⊏E⊐ ⊏F⊐ ⊏G⊐ ⊏H⊐ ⊏I⊐ ⊏J⊐ ⊏K⊐ ⊏L⊐ ⊏M⊐ ⊏N⊐ ⊏O⊐ ⊏P⊐ ⊏Q⊐ ⊏R⊐ ⊏S⊐ ⊏T⊐ ⊏U⊐ ⊏V⊐ ⊏W⊐ ⊏X⊐ ⊏Y⊐ ⊏Z⊐
⊏A⊐ ⊏B⊐ ⊏C⊐ ⊏D⊐ ⊏E⊐ ⊏F⊐ ⊏G⊐ ⊏H⊐ ⊏I⊐ ⊏J⊐ ⊏K⊐ ⊏L⊐ ⊏M⊐ ⊏N⊐ ⊏O⊐ ⊏P⊐ ⊏Q⊐ ⊏R⊐ ⊏S⊐ ⊏T⊐ ⊏U⊐ ⊏V⊐ ⊏W⊐ ⊏X⊐ ⊏Y⊐ ⊏Z⊐

4
⊏A⊐ ⊏B⊐ ⊏C⊐ ⊏D⊐ ⊏E⊐ ⊏F⊐ ⊏G⊐ ⊏H⊐ ⊏I⊐ ⊏J⊐ ⊏K⊐ ⊏L⊐ ⊏M⊐ ⊏N⊐ ⊏O⊐ ⊏P⊐ ⊏Q⊐ ⊏R⊐ ⊏S⊐ ⊏T⊐ ⊏U⊐ ⊏V⊐ ⊏W⊐ ⊏X⊐ ⊏Y⊐ ⊏Z⊐
⊏A⊐ ⊏B⊐ ⊏C⊐ ⊏D⊐ ⊏E⊐ ⊏F⊐ ⊏G⊐ ⊏H⊐ ⊏I⊐ ⊏J⊐ ⊏K⊐ ⊏L⊐ ⊏M⊐ ⊏N⊐ ⊏O⊐ ⊏P⊐ ⊏Q⊐ ⊏R⊐ ⊏S⊐ ⊏T⊐ ⊏U⊐ ⊏V⊐ ⊏W⊐ ⊏X⊐ ⊏Y⊐ ⊏Z⊐

	DESCRIPTIVE ITEMS—Individual and Organizational Values		CODE NAME 1	CODE NAME 2	CODE NAME 3	CODE NAME 4
U	1 Individual financial success, personal prominence and power	1	⊏R⊐ ⊏S⊐ ⊏O⊐	⊏R⊐ ⊏S⊐ ⊏O⊐	⊏R⊐ ⊏S⊐ ⊏O⊐	⊏R⊐ ⊏S⊐ ⊏O⊐
UP	2 Popularity and social success, being liked and admired	2	⊏R⊐ ⊏S⊐ ⊏O⊐	⊏R⊐ ⊏S⊐ ⊏O⊐	⊏R⊐ ⊏S⊐ ⊏O⊐	⊏R⊐ ⊏S⊐ ⊏O⊐
UPF	3 Active teamwork toward common goals, organizational unity	3	⊏R⊐ ⊏S⊐ ⊏O⊐	⊏R⊐ ⊏S⊐ ⊏O⊐	⊏R⊐ ⊏S⊐ ⊏O⊐	⊏R⊐ ⊏S⊐ ⊏O⊐
UF	4 Efficiency, strong impartial management	4	⊏R⊐ ⊏S⊐ ⊏O⊐	⊏R⊐ ⊏S⊐ ⊏O⊐	⊏R⊐ ⊏S⊐ ⊏O⊐	⊏R⊐ ⊏S⊐ ⊏O⊐
UNF	5 Active reinforcement of authority, rules, and regulations	5	⊏R⊐ ⊏S⊐ ⊏O⊐	⊏R⊐ ⊏S⊐ ⊏O⊐	⊏R⊐ ⊏S⊐ ⊏O⊐	⊏R⊐ ⊏S⊐ ⊏O⊐
UN	6 Tough-minded, self-oriented assertiveness	6	⊏R⊐ ⊏S⊐ ⊏O⊐	⊏R⊐ ⊏S⊐ ⊏O⊐	⊏R⊐ ⊏S⊐ ⊏O⊐	⊏R⊐ ⊏S⊐ ⊏O⊐
UNB	7 Rugged, self-oriented individualism, resistance to authority	7	⊏R⊐ ⊏S⊐ ⊏O⊐	⊏R⊐ ⊏S⊐ ⊏O⊐	⊏R⊐ ⊏S⊐ ⊏O⊐	⊏R⊐ ⊏S⊐ ⊏O⊐
UB	8 Having a good time, releasing tension, relaxing control	8	⊏R⊐ ⊏S⊐ ⊏O⊐	⊏R⊐ ⊏S⊐ ⊏O⊐	⊏R⊐ ⊏S⊐ ⊏O⊐	⊏R⊐ ⊏S⊐ ⊏O⊐
UPB	9 Protecting less able members, providing help when needed	9	⊏R⊐ ⊏S⊐ ⊏O⊐	⊏R⊐ ⊏S⊐ ⊏O⊐	⊏R⊐ ⊏S⊐ ⊏O⊐	⊏R⊐ ⊏S⊐ ⊏O⊐
P	10 Equality, democratic participation in decision making	10	⊏R⊐ ⊏S⊐ ⊏O⊐	⊏R⊐ ⊏S⊐ ⊏O⊐	⊏R⊐ ⊏S⊐ ⊏O⊐	⊏R⊐ ⊏S⊐ ⊏O⊐
PF	11 Responsible idealism, collaborative work	11	⊏R⊐ ⊏S⊐ ⊏O⊐	⊏R⊐ ⊏S⊐ ⊏O⊐	⊏R⊐ ⊏S⊐ ⊏O⊐	⊏R⊐ ⊏S⊐ ⊏O⊐
F	12 Conservative, established, "correct" ways of doing things	12	⊏R⊐ ⊏S⊐ ⊏O⊐	⊏R⊐ ⊏S⊐ ⊏O⊐	⊏R⊐ ⊏S⊐ ⊏O⊐	⊏R⊐ ⊏S⊐ ⊏O⊐
NF	13 Restraining individual desires for organizational goals	13	⊏R⊐ ⊏S⊐ ⊏O⊐	⊏R⊐ ⊏S⊐ ⊏O⊐	⊏R⊐ ⊏S⊐ ⊏O⊐	⊏R⊐ ⊏S⊐ ⊏O⊐
N	14 Self-protection, self-interest first, self-sufficiency	14	⊏R⊐ ⊏S⊐ ⊏O⊐	⊏R⊐ ⊏S⊐ ⊏O⊐	⊏R⊐ ⊏S⊐ ⊏O⊐	⊏R⊐ ⊏S⊐ ⊏O⊐
NB	15 Rejection of established procedures, rejection of conformity	15	⊏R⊐ ⊏S⊐ ⊏O⊐	⊏R⊐ ⊏S⊐ ⊏O⊐	⊏R⊐ ⊏S⊐ ⊏O⊐	⊏R⊐ ⊏S⊐ ⊏O⊐
B	16 Change to new procedures, different values, creativity	16	⊏R⊐ ⊏S⊐ ⊏O⊐	⊏R⊐ ⊏S⊐ ⊏O⊐	⊏R⊐ ⊏S⊐ ⊏O⊐	⊏R⊐ ⊏S⊐ ⊏O⊐
PB	17 Friendship, mutual pleasure, recreation	17	⊏R⊐ ⊏S⊐ ⊏O⊐	⊏R⊐ ⊏S⊐ ⊏O⊐	⊏R⊐ ⊏S⊐ ⊏O⊐	⊏R⊐ ⊏S⊐ ⊏O⊐
DP	18 Trust in the goodness of others	18	⊏R⊐ ⊏S⊐ ⊏O⊐	⊏R⊐ ⊏S⊐ ⊏O⊐	⊏R⊐ ⊏S⊐ ⊏O⊐	⊏R⊐ ⊏S⊐ ⊏O⊐
DPF	19 Dedication, faithfulness, loyalty to the organization	19	⊏R⊐ ⊏S⊐ ⊏O⊐	⊏R⊐ ⊏S⊐ ⊏O⊐	⊏R⊐ ⊏S⊐ ⊏O⊐	⊏R⊐ ⊏S⊐ ⊏O⊐
DF	20 Obedience to the chain of command, complying with authority	20	⊏R⊐ ⊏S⊐ ⊏O⊐	⊏R⊐ ⊏S⊐ ⊏O⊐	⊏R⊐ ⊏S⊐ ⊏O⊐	⊏R⊐ ⊏S⊐ ⊏O⊐
DNF	21 Self-sacrifice if necessary to reach organizational goals	21	⊏R⊐ ⊏S⊐ ⊏O⊐	⊏R⊐ ⊏S⊐ ⊏O⊐	⊏R⊐ ⊏S⊐ ⊏O⊐	⊏R⊐ ⊏S⊐ ⊏O⊐
DN	22 Passive rejection of popularity, going it alone	22	⊏R⊐ ⊏S⊐ ⊏O⊐	⊏R⊐ ⊏S⊐ ⊏O⊐	⊏R⊐ ⊏S⊐ ⊏O⊐	⊏R⊐ ⊏S⊐ ⊏O⊐
DNB	23 Admission of failure, withdrawal of effort	23	⊏R⊐ ⊏S⊐ ⊏O⊐	⊏R⊐ ⊏S⊐ ⊏O⊐	⊏R⊐ ⊏S⊐ ⊏O⊐	⊏R⊐ ⊏S⊐ ⊏O⊐
DB	24 Passive non-cooperation with authority	24	⊏R⊐ ⊏S⊐ ⊏O⊐	⊏R⊐ ⊏S⊐ ⊏O⊐	⊏R⊐ ⊏S⊐ ⊏O⊐	⊏R⊐ ⊏S⊐ ⊏O⊐
DPB	25 Quiet contentment, taking it easy	25	⊏R⊐ ⊏S⊐ ⊏O⊐	⊏R⊐ ⊏S⊐ ⊏O⊐	⊏R⊐ ⊏S⊐ ⊏O⊐	⊏R⊐ ⊏S⊐ ⊏O⊐
D	26 Giving up personal needs and desires, passivity	26	⊏R⊐ ⊏S⊐ ⊏O⊐	⊏R⊐ ⊏S⊐ ⊏O⊐	⊏R⊐ ⊏S⊐ ⊏O⊐	⊏R⊐ ⊏S⊐ ⊏O⊐

R = RARELY   S = SOMETIMES   O = OFTEN

Source: Reprinted by permission of SYMLOG Consulting Group.

127

Figure 11.3
Behavior Form, Answer Sheet

ANSWER SHEET

QUESTION # ...   c1ɔ c2ɔ c3ɔ c4ɔ c5ɔ c6ɔ c7ɔ c8ɔ c9ɔ   cAɔ cBɔ cCɔ cDɔ cEɔ cFɔ cGɔ cHɔ

Rater's Code Name: (3 vertical letters)

cAɔ cBɔ cCɔ cDɔ cEɔ cFɔ cGɔ cHɔ cIɔ cJɔ cKɔ cLɔ cMɔ cNɔ cOɔ cPɔ cQɔ cRɔ cSɔ cTɔ cUɔ cVɔ cWɔ cXɔ cYɔ cZɔ
cAɔ cBɔ cCɔ cDɔ cEɔ cFɔ cGɔ cHɔ cIɔ cJɔ cKɔ cLɔ cMɔ cNɔ cOɔ cPɔ cQɔ cRɔ cSɔ cTɔ cUɔ cVɔ cWɔ cXɔ cYɔ cZɔ
cAɔ cBɔ cCɔ cDɔ cEɔ cFɔ cGɔ cHɔ cIɔ cJɔ cKɔ cLɔ cMɔ cNɔ cOɔ cPɔ cQɔ cRɔ cSɔ cTɔ cUɔ cVɔ cWɔ cXɔ cYɔ cZɔ

Code Name of Persons or Concepts Rated: (3 vertical letter code names)

1 cAɔ cBɔ cCɔ cDɔ cEɔ cFɔ cGɔ cHɔ cIɔ cJɔ cKɔ cLɔ cMɔ cNɔ cOɔ cPɔ cQɔ cRɔ cSɔ cTɔ cUɔ cVɔ cWɔ cXɔ cYɔ cZɔ
cAɔ cBɔ cCɔ cDɔ cEɔ cFɔ cGɔ cHɔ cIɔ cJɔ cKɔ cLɔ cMɔ cNɔ cOɔ cPɔ cQɔ cRɔ cSɔ cTɔ cUɔ cVɔ cWɔ cXɔ cYɔ cZɔ
cAɔ cBɔ cCɔ cDɔ cEɔ cFɔ cGɔ cHɔ cIɔ cJɔ cKɔ cLɔ cMɔ cNɔ cOɔ cPɔ cQɔ cRɔ cSɔ cTɔ cUɔ cVɔ cWɔ cXɔ cYɔ cZɔ

2 cAɔ cBɔ cCɔ cDɔ cEɔ cFɔ cGɔ cHɔ cIɔ cJɔ cKɔ cLɔ cMɔ cNɔ cOɔ cPɔ cQɔ cRɔ cSɔ cTɔ cUɔ cVɔ cWɔ cXɔ cYɔ cZɔ
cAɔ cBɔ cCɔ cDɔ cEɔ cFɔ cGɔ cHɔ cIɔ cJɔ cKɔ cLɔ cMɔ cNɔ cOɔ cPɔ cQɔ cRɔ cSɔ cTɔ cUɔ cVɔ cWɔ cXɔ cYɔ cZɔ
cAɔ cBɔ cCɔ cDɔ cEɔ cFɔ cGɔ cHɔ cIɔ cJɔ cKɔ cLɔ cMɔ cNɔ cOɔ cPɔ cQɔ cRɔ cSɔ cTɔ cUɔ cVɔ cWɔ cXɔ cYɔ cZɔ

3 cAɔ cBɔ cCɔ cDɔ cEɔ cFɔ cGɔ cHɔ cIɔ cJɔ cKɔ cLɔ cMɔ cNɔ cOɔ cPɔ cQɔ cRɔ cSɔ cTɔ cUɔ cVɔ cWɔ cXɔ cYɔ cZɔ
cAɔ cBɔ cCɔ cDɔ cEɔ cFɔ cGɔ cHɔ cIɔ cJɔ cKɔ cLɔ cMɔ cNɔ cOɔ cPɔ cQɔ cRɔ cSɔ cTɔ cUɔ cVɔ cWɔ cXɔ cYɔ cZɔ
cAɔ cBɔ cCɔ cDɔ cEɔ cFɔ cGɔ cHɔ cIɔ cJɔ cKɔ cLɔ cMɔ cNɔ cOɔ cPɔ cQɔ cRɔ cSɔ cTɔ cUɔ cVɔ cWɔ cXɔ cYɔ cZɔ

4 cAɔ cBɔ cCɔ cDɔ cEɔ cFɔ cGɔ cHɔ cIɔ cJɔ cKɔ cLɔ cMɔ cNɔ cOɔ cPɔ cQɔ cRɔ cSɔ cTɔ cUɔ cVɔ cWɔ cXɔ cYɔ cZɔ
cAɔ cBɔ cCɔ cDɔ cEɔ cFɔ cGɔ cHɔ cIɔ cJɔ cKɔ cLɔ cMɔ cNɔ cOɔ cPɔ cQɔ cRɔ cSɔ cTɔ cUɔ cVɔ cWɔ cXɔ cYɔ cZɔ
cAɔ cBɔ cCɔ cDɔ cEɔ cFɔ cGɔ cHɔ cIɔ cJɔ cKɔ cLɔ cMɔ cNɔ cOɔ cPɔ cQɔ cRɔ cSɔ cTɔ cUɔ cVɔ cWɔ cXɔ cYɔ cZɔ

DESCRIPTIVE ITEMS – Behavior Form Copyright © 1987 by Robert F. Bales

		CODE NAME 1	CODE NAME 2	CODE NAME 3	CODE NAME 4
U	1 Dominant, active, talkative	cRɔ cSɔ cOɔ	cRɔ cSɔ cOɔ	cRɔ cSɔ cOɔ	cRɔ cSɔ cOɔ
UP	2 Outgoing, sociable, extroverted	cRɔ cSɔ cOɔ	cRɔ cSɔ cOɔ	cRɔ cSɔ cOɔ	cRɔ cSɔ cOɔ
UPF	3 Persuasive, convincing, shows task leadership	cRɔ cSɔ cOɔ	cRɔ cSɔ cOɔ	cRɔ cSɔ cOɔ	cRɔ cSɔ cOɔ
UF	4 Business-like, decisive, impersonal	cRɔ cSɔ cOɔ	cRɔ cSɔ cOɔ	cRɔ cSɔ cOɔ	cRɔ cSɔ cOɔ
UNF	5 Strict, demanding, controlling	cRɔ cSɔ cOɔ	cRɔ cSɔ cOɔ	cRɔ cSɔ cOɔ	cRɔ cSɔ cOɔ
UN	6 Tough, competitive, aggressive	cRɔ cSɔ cOɔ	cRɔ cSɔ cOɔ	cRɔ cSɔ cOɔ	cRɔ cSɔ cOɔ
UNB	7 Rebellious, unruly, self-centered	cRɔ cSɔ cOɔ	cRɔ cSɔ cOɔ	cRɔ cSɔ cOɔ	cRɔ cSɔ cOɔ
UB	8 Joking, witty, clever	cRɔ cSɔ cOɔ	cRɔ cSɔ cOɔ	cRɔ cSɔ cOɔ	cRɔ cSɔ cOɔ
UPB	9 Protects others, sympathetic, nurturant	cRɔ cSɔ cOɔ	cRɔ cSɔ cOɔ	cRɔ cSɔ cOɔ	cRɔ cSɔ cOɔ
P	10 Friendly, democratic, group-oriented	cRɔ cSɔ cOɔ	cRɔ cSɔ cOɔ	cRɔ cSɔ cOɔ	cRɔ cSɔ cOɔ
PF	11 Cooperative, reasonable, constructive	cRɔ cSɔ cOɔ	cRɔ cSɔ cOɔ	cRɔ cSɔ cOɔ	cRɔ cSɔ cOɔ
F	12 Serious, logical, objective	cRɔ cSɔ cOɔ	cRɔ cSɔ cOɔ	cRɔ cSɔ cOɔ	cRɔ cSɔ cOɔ
NF	13 Rule-oriented, insistent, inflexible	cRɔ cSɔ cOɔ	cRɔ cSɔ cOɔ	cRɔ cSɔ cOɔ	cRɔ cSɔ cOɔ
N	14 Self-protective, unfriendly, negativistic	cRɔ cSɔ cOɔ	cRɔ cSɔ cOɔ	cRɔ cSɔ cOɔ	cRɔ cSɔ cOɔ
NB	15 Uncooperative, pessimistic, cynical	cRɔ cSɔ cOɔ	cRɔ cSɔ cOɔ	cRɔ cSɔ cOɔ	cRɔ cSɔ cOɔ
B	16 Expresses emotions, shows feelings	cRɔ cSɔ cOɔ	cRɔ cSɔ cOɔ	cRɔ cSɔ cOɔ	cRɔ cSɔ cOɔ
PB	17 Likeable, affectionate, enjoyable	cRɔ cSɔ cOɔ	cRɔ cSɔ cOɔ	cRɔ cSɔ cOɔ	cRɔ cSɔ cOɔ
DP	18 Trustful, accepting, sensitive	cRɔ cSɔ cOɔ	cRɔ cSɔ cOɔ	cRɔ cSɔ cOɔ	cRɔ cSɔ cOɔ
DPF	19 Modest, respectful, dedicated	cRɔ cSɔ cOɔ	cRɔ cSɔ cOɔ	cRɔ cSɔ cOɔ	cRɔ cSɔ cOɔ
DF	20 Cautious, dutiful, obedient	cRɔ cSɔ cOɔ	cRɔ cSɔ cOɔ	cRɔ cSɔ cOɔ	cRɔ cSɔ cOɔ
DNF	21 Constrained, conforming, self-sacrificing	cRɔ cSɔ cOɔ	cRɔ cSɔ cOɔ	cRɔ cSɔ cOɔ	cRɔ cSɔ cOɔ
DN	22 Depressed, unsociable, resentful	cRɔ cSɔ cOɔ	cRɔ cSɔ cOɔ	cRɔ cSɔ cOɔ	cRɔ cSɔ cOɔ
DNB	23 Alienated, rejects task, withdraws	cRɔ cSɔ cOɔ	cRɔ cSɔ cOɔ	cRɔ cSɔ cOɔ	cRɔ cSɔ cOɔ
DB	24 Indecisive, anxious, holds back	cRɔ cSɔ cOɔ	cRɔ cSɔ cOɔ	cRɔ cSɔ cOɔ	cRɔ cSɔ cOɔ
DPB	25 Quietly contented, satisfied, unconcerned	cRɔ cSɔ cOɔ	cRɔ cSɔ cOɔ	cRɔ cSɔ cOɔ	cRɔ cSɔ cOɔ
D	26 Silent, passive, uninvolved	cRɔ cSɔ cOɔ	cRɔ cSɔ cOɔ	cRɔ cSɔ cOɔ	cRɔ cSɔ cOɔ

R = RARELY   S = SOMETIMES   O = OFTEN

Source: Reprinted by permission of SYMLOG Consulting Group.

The data collected from the twenty-six-item questionnaire can be summarized in the form of a bar graph for the detailed analysis of the performance of a single individual, as rated by other members of a team, or of a set of persons holding a given role. This bar graph can be compared with "norms" for effective performance for a team member or a particular role. For example, Bachman (1988) reports SYMLOG ratings from a study of U.S. Naval commanders of "average" and "superior" commands on active duty in the Atlantic and Pacific Fleets. The data were collected as part of a larger study by McBer and Company and represent a sample of twelve commands: two average and two superior commands from each of the three naval communities (air, surface, and submarine). As a sample of the results, a bar graph for the aggregated behavior of all superior COs compared with SYMLOG Consulting Group norms is given in Figure 11.4. The "x"s on the bar graph indicate the extent to which the list of behaviors was observed by members of the command (rarely, sometimes, or often). The "E"s, connected by a solid line, represent a norm based on thousands of questionnaires for managers of organizations, primarily in business.

Compared with the business managers, the superior naval COs showed more of the behavior associated with an extroverted, purposeful, democratic task leader and less of a tendency to be legalistic and self-punishing. Bachman also reports the average behavior of COs in average commands and the behavior of executive officers, junior officers, and enlisted ranks in both superior and average commands.

The most recent version of the SYMLOG field theory developed by Bales is not published in the form of a text but is represented in a series of computer programs that provide an analysis for the bar graph compared with norms for effective leadership and team work. These programs are available to consultants associated with the SYMLOG Consulting Group located in San Diego, California. In brief, the program that provides an analysis of a bar graph produces a report of some ten pages or more indicating which of the values or behaviors that have been rated are at an optimal level for effective teamwork, which are under- or overrepresented, which are necessary sometimes but dangerous, and which almost always interfere with teamwork.

Although the computer-based analysis of the bar graphs goes well beyond the type of data represented in other leadership behavior checklists in current use, the major advantage of the SYMLOG approach, not found in other management assessment systems, is the ability of the theory to provide a picture of the images of team members in a three-dimensional interpersonal space. This picture is in the form of a field diagram (see Figure 11.5). The field diagram included here is not based on ratings by an actual team member, but rather has been devised to illustrate the type of analysis of value ratings available in the current version of the field theory.

Figure 11.4
Aggregated Behavior of All Superior COs (x's) Compared with SCG Norms (E's)

SCG Frequency Bargraph of General Behaviors
Based on the ratings made on: Your Group

Type: UPF   Final Location: 6U 9P 6F
E = optimum location for most effective
x = the average rating on each item

		RARELY	SOMETIMES	OFTEN
1 U	Active, dominant, talks a lot	xxxxxxxxxxxxxxxxxxxxxxxxExx		
2 UP	Extroverted, outgoing, positive	xxxxxxxxxxxxxxxxxxxxxxxxxExxxx		
3 UPF	A purposeful democratic task leader	xxxxxxxxxxxxxxxxxxxxxExxxx		
4 UF	An assertive business-like manager	xxxxxxxxxxxxxxxxxxxxxxxxxxxExx		
5 UNF	Authoritarian, controlling, disapproving	xxxxxxxxxxxxxExx		
6 UN	Domineering, tough-minded, powerful	xxxxxxxxxxxxxExx		
7 UNB	Provocative, egocentric, shows off	xxxx E		
8 UB	Jokes around, expressive, dramatic	xxxxxxxxxxxxxxxE		
9 UPB	Entertaining, sociable, smiling, warm	xxxxxxxxxxxxxxxxxxxxxExxxx		
10 P	Friendly, equalitarian	xxxxxxxxxxxxxxxxxxxxxxxxExxx		
11 PF	Works cooperatively with others	xxxxxxxxxxxxxxxxxxxxxxxxxxxDx		
12 F	Analytical, task-oriented, problem-solving	xxxxxxxxxxxxxxxxxxxxxxxxxxxExxxx		
13 NF	Legalistic, has to be right	xxxxxxxxxxxx E		
14 N	Unfriendly, negativistic	xE		
15 NB	Irritable, cynical, won't cooperate	xE		
16 B	Shows feelings and emotions	xxxxxxxxxxxxxxE		
17 PB	Affectionate, likeable, fun to be with	xxxxxxxxxxxxxxxxxxxExx		
18 DP	Looks up to others, appreciative, trustful	xxxxxxxxxxxxxxxxxxxxExx		
19 DPF	Gentle, willing to accept responsibility	xxxxxxxxxxxxxxxxxxxxxxxxxxExx		
20 DF	Obedient, works submissively	xxxxxxxxxxxx E		
21 DNF	Self-punishing, works too hard	xxxxxxxxxx E		
22 DN	Depressed, sad, resentful, rejecting	E		
23 DNB	Alienated, quits, withdraws	E		
24 DB	Afraid to try, doubts own ability	E		
25 DPB	Quietly happy just to be with others	xxxxxxxxxxE		
26 D	Passive, introverted, says little	xEx		

Source: Based on *SYMLOG: A System for the Multiple Level Observation of Groups*, by Robert F. Bales and Stephen P. Cohen with the assistance of Stephen A. Williamson, p. 21. Copyright © 1979 by The Free Press, a Division of Macmillan, Inc. Reprinted by permission of the publisher.

Notes: Type: UPF; Final Location: 6U   9P   6F
E = optimum location for most effective; x = the average rating on each item;
B = backward; D = downward; F = forward; N = negative; P = positive;
U = upward

Figure 11.5
A Sample of an Individual Field Diagram

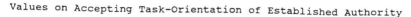

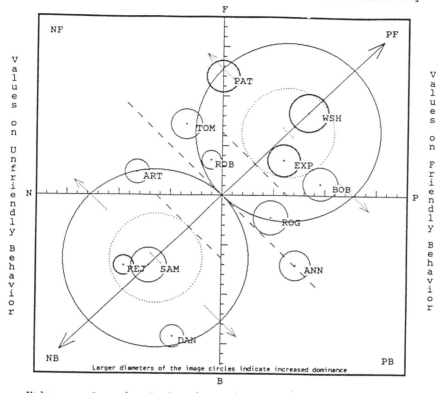

Values on Accepting Task-Orientation of Established Authority

Larger diameters of the image circles indicate increased dominance

Values on Opposing Task-Orientation of Established Authority

Source: From Robert F. Bales, "Bales Report," presented at the SYMLOG Users' Conference, San Diego, CA, September 1989. Reprinted by permission of SYMLOG Consulting Group.

Notes: EXP = expect self to be seen by others; REJ = reject; WSH = wish to show; B = backward; F = forward; N = negative; P = positive

In the field diagram, the horizontal axis represents the Positive-Negative dimension and the vertical axis the Forward-Backward dimension. These are the two dimensions that are most central for the analysis of the extent to which the "image" (summary position based on the twenty-six-item checklist) of an individual or concept is in the most effective position. The positions of images on these two dimensions also have the most relevance for determining whether or not the members of a team are unified, holding a common set of values, or polarized. The third dimension, Upward-Downward, is represented by the size of the circle surrounding the dot that locates the center of the image. The larger the circle, the more dominant the image.

To derive a summary location for an image, the twenty-six-item checklist is scored by adding all the ratings of the items containing vectors indicating values (or behavior) for one end of a dimension and subtracting the sum of the ratings of items representing vectors indicating values at the other end. For example, the first nine items on the questionnaire (see left-hand column on Figure 11.2) all contain an element of U (Upward values). The first item represents a value on pure "U," the second item an Upward-Positive value, the third item an Upward-Positive-Forward value, and so on. The last nine items on the checklist all contain some element of Downward values. When the response "rarely" is scored as 0, "sometimes" as 1, and "often" as 2, the resulting Upward or Downward score can range from 0 to 18. The same scoring procedure is used for each of the other two dimensions.

The field diagram in Figure 11.5 represents the position of team members and certain key concepts, as they might appear to a leader or to one member of a team. If this were an actual team, the leader would have a very difficult time with coordination, since only a few of the members come close to being in the optimal location. As a result of administering thousands of questionnaires to leaders and members of effective teams, it has been observed that the location of the values that an effective leader (or member) would WISH for, indicated as WSH on the field diagram, is Upward, Positive, and Forward. The location of the values such a person would REJECT (REJ) is Downward, Negative, and Backward. For a person with this combination of WISH and REJECT images, the most common direction of polarization in the group is along the line passing through the WISH image and the center of the field diagram at an angle of 45 degrees to the Positive-Negative axis.

Two large circles are drawn on the field diagram with centers on this "Line of Polarization" and tangent to each other at the center of the field diagram. The dashed line, through the center of the diagram and perpendicular to the Line of Polarization, represents the "Line of Balance." If all of the images of team members lie within the large circle in the WISH (Positive-Forward) quadrant of the diagram, the individual rater sees the team as unified within an effective set of values. Those members whose images lie within the smaller, dotted, "inner circle" are most likely to be leaders or other key members of the team. In contrast, images that lie on the opposite side of the Line of Balance, in the Negative-Backward quadrant, are seen as being members of a subgroup that is polarized with regard to the most effective subgroup. The small dotted arrows, shown at the edges of the large circles, represent the likeliest direction of secondary polarization, should it appear. For example, in the sample field diagram, unless the leader pays close attention to coordination, PAT may move off in a Negative-Forward direction and BOB in a Positive-Backward direction.

Bales has developed a computer program for the analysis of an individual's view of a team as indicated on a field diagram. This program is more detailed than any existing text or program for group analysis. Although Bales has provided elaborate appendices to earlier books (Bales, 1970; Bales & Cohen, 1979) that described the values, behavior, and other characteristics of the twenty-six personality/behavior types, it was left to the reader to match the team members with the specific types and to infer how they might interact with each other. With the present computer program, once an observer has rated a set of team members, the computer calculates the locations of the images and plots them on a field diagram, as in Figure 11.5, and then produces a "Bales Report," ranging from thirty to fifty pages in length, depending upon the number of persons in the team.

The report summarizes the characteristics of each of the team members and indicates how they would be expected to react to the other team members. In addition, the report gives suggestions to the team leader concerning strategies for developing a more effective team and indicates how an "optimum leader" might relate to each of the members. As an indication of the detailed information in the report, several pages are included here from the Bales Report to PAT based on PAT's ratings of BOB, who could be an effective team member, and SAM, who is likely to make trouble for any task-oriented leader. (See sample pages in Figure 11.6.)

Figure 11.6
A Sample of Bales's Report on an Individual Field Diagram

```
         This Section is about the following member or members:

                                  BOB

AS SEEN BY THE RATER THE MOST CHARACTERISTIC VALUES APPEAR TO BE:


                      POPULARITY AND SOCIAL SUCCESS,
                   TEAMWORK TOWARD SOCIAL SOLIDARITY


      GENERAL DESCRIPTION OF INDIVIDUALS WHO SHOW THESE VALUES

Members with this kind of personality show active, friendly,
outgoing social behavior.  They tend to be confident and feel
highly involved, strong and able to lead the group toward goals
of equality and integrated teamwork.  Usually, however, they are
more interested in receiving liking and admiration from a
friendly group than in structuring and performing the demanding
tasks of the group.  Their activity tends to be "political" in
nature.  They tend to attract attention, to be well liked, and
are often successful in "popular elections" of any kind.
```

Figure 11.6 *(continued)*

HOW BOB MIGHT FIT INTO AN ACTUAL "MOST EFFECTIVE TEAM"

BOB This person, if correctly perceived, would fit well into a
"most effective team." However, the main contribution would
be to team solidarity. There would probably be only
marginal contribution to the work of the task.

DIFFERENCES from the "most effective" location:
         DOMINANCE: 0.0
         FRIENDLINESS: + 3.2
         TASK WORK: - 5.2

HOW BOB MIGHT RELATE TO OTHER MEMBERS

The values of members on the individualistic unfriendly side,
such as PAT, TOM, ART, SAM, and DAN, are very apt to provoke
polarizations, either among themselves, or with members on the
friendly social side. Such members may actually intend to be
unfriendly, in order to feel more safe -- better able to defend
themselves and resist subtle pressure toward cooperation when
they are in a clearly dissenting minority. They are likely to
increase their dissent, their resentment and resistance, when
confronted with members such as BOB who may well be successful
social leaders, with popularity, status, and power in the main
group.

Members like ANN tend to oppose authority and task demands.
Members like BOB are not strongly supportive of authority or task
demands, but nevertheless, they probably will dislike and tend to
polarize against the disruptive attitudes and tactics of ANN.
(If one of the disruptive members is a successful joker, who
amuses the group, he or she may be a partial exception.

Attitudes toward a joker are likely to be mixed, but a successful
joker is not likely to be regarded in the same way as serious
objectors are.)

Members like ROG are somewhat similar to members such as BOB in
their dominant, sociable, extroverted needs, and may compete for
popularity and social emotional leadership in the group.
However, members like ROG are probably even less task oriented
than BOB and more likely to feel negative about authority, or at
least about conservatism. Consequently, they may be more
attractive than members such as BOB as leaders of any very
liberal subgroup within the group.

Members like ROG and ROB are only weakly friendly, if at all, and
are not oriented to the task. They are apt to be felt as a kind
of dead weight on teamwork. In general, they may be confused,
with mixed feelings about most issues and values. They may,
however, be open to persuasion in some cases, and members like
BOB may be as likely as any members to be able to exercise some
persuasion, at least in the direction of more friendliness. An
optimum leader will try to encourage such persuasive efforts,
particularly on issues that are closely contested. Members like
ROG and ROB may hold a "swing vote" on such issues.

Figure 11.6 *(continued)*

HOW AN "OPTIMUM LEADER" MIGHT RELATE TO BOB

An optimum leader would probably find members like BOB lively, interesting and attractive, although they are less task oriented than optimum, and perhaps too much oriented to personal popularity. However, they may also be important as social leaders who help to maintain friendliness and good feeling in the group. It is vitally important for an optimum leader to build strong bridges between task leaders and social leaders. Members such as BOB may be more attractive and influential than task leaders, including optimum leaders. An optimum leader should recognize their importance, and solicit their help in leadership. Otherwise, one of more of them may become the leader of a faction that splits off from the rest of the main team toward the more liberal side.

****

This Section is about the following member or members:

SAM

AS SEEN BY THE RATER THE MOST CHARACTERISTIC VALUES APPEAR TO BE:

RUGGED, SELF ORIENTED INDIVIDUALISM,
RESISTANCE TO AUTHORITY

GENERAL DESCRIPTION OF INDIVIDUALS WHO SHOW THESE VALUES

These values are often shown by actual or symbolic attacks ridiculing conventionality and submissive dependence on the part of other group members. There are constant attempts to display the self as fascinating, amazing, shocking, unrestrained, spectacular, and mysterious -- to attract attention and admiration by extravagant and egocentric mannerisms, dress, or speech. The implication is that other group members are colorless, spineless "wimps."

A companion theme seems to be to show that one is powerful and independent, that one can not be controlled by established authority, that those in authority are ineffective -- unable to punish deviance, unable to defend themselves, unable to protect group members who are submissive and dependent on authority. Revolutionary or heretical political, social, or religious values are sometimes displayed as a part of the self picture. The rebel implicitly presents himself or herself as a better leader, and looks for submissive recruits who are also alienated from the main group.

HOW SAM MIGHT FIT INTO AN ACTUAL "MOST EFFECTIVE TEAM"

SAM What can be done about this kind of individual? (One needs to be sure the ratings are essentially accurate.) But the ratings indicate a dominating, unrelenting tendency to attack conformity and conventionality of almost any kind.

135

Figure 11.6 *(continued)*

Teamwork with such an individual would be impossible, although a part of the time he or she may only lie in wait for a strategic opportunity to attack.

DIFFERENCES from the "most effective" location:
```
DOMINANCE:       + 1.0
FRIENDLINESS:    -13.6
TASK WORK:       -13.6
```

HOW SAM MIGHT RELATE TO OTHER MEMBERS

Ordinarily, most members of the group, in this case, BOB and PAT, will be included in the array of members who are likely to be opposed and attacked by members like SAM. In general, members like SAM will tend to oppose and develop active polarized conflicts with both liberal and conservative factions and subgroups, as well as the mainstream team. In most cases, the conflicts will center on the leaders of the mainstream group, and the various factions, if any. The submissive members who are most likely to be held in contempt and ridiculed by SAM are those who are closest to the leader or principal leaders of the group.

Members such as TOM are the most dominant and authoritarian elements in the group, and are the most likely targets of the rebellious attack by members like SAM. A polarization of this kind is analogous to that between the far right and the far left in a political context. Such a polarization tends to be bitter, chronic, and intractable in the context of small groups, as it is in the larger society.

Submissive members, perhaps especially those on the unfriendly side, such as ART and DAN, who are likely to be isolated, rejected, or otherwise vulnerable, may submit to the attacks and sometimes persuasive arguments of rebellious members such as SAM, from fear or from hope of relief, or even hope of protection if they submit. In general, the vulnerable members may include submissive authoritarians as well as submissive anti-authoritarians.

In extreme cases, where a rebellious anti-authoritarian enforcer or subgroup is actually able to force one or more others to submit abjectly and repeatedly by threatening and punishing them, and perhaps by preventing their escape, such victims may finally "identify with the aggressor" in a desperate attempt to preserve some fantasy picture of the self as having some safety, or power and status. They may become psychological "slaves", bound by paradoxically strong bonds to the enforcer, in a vicious circle of interaction that is full of conflict, victimization, and self-pitying complaint, but is, nevertheless, self-maintaining and persistent in spite of opportunities the victims may have to escape.

If a sufficient number of members (even a very disparate array of negative and anti-authoritarian values, and even including those with authoritarian values) are unhappy enough about the way things are going in the group, it may be that, in spite of great value differences among them, they can be assembled into an effective opposition by a leader or leaders of the "revolutionary" type, such as SAM and by temporary cooperation, they may succeed in bringing about a "revolution".

Figure 11.6 *(continued)*

If hostility toward established authority in the group is very widespread and strong, then others in addition to the chronically alienated members, such as ROB, BOB, and ROG, may regard hostile attitudes and actions against established authority as friendly and protective toward themselves. In this case, they may suppress negative feelings toward members such as SAM who may be leading a rebellion, and begin to regard them as heroes of the revolution.

If a revolution succeeds, a "new order" and a new definition of legitimate authority and accepted group tasks is set up. A "new era" in terms of accepted values and norms begins. A new majority of the group may become unified under the new leadership. The former authority, if still present, is attacked as an "enemy of the revolution," and a purge of former adherents of authority sets in.

HOW AN "OPTIMUM LEADER" MIGHT RELATE TO SAM

If members such as SAM are isolated, it may be possible for an optimum leader to encourage and maintain a tolerance for SAM on the part of other members. In some cases, rebels such as SAM eventually wear out everybody's patience and face nearly unanimous opposition by other members. This is possibly the solution that inflicts the least damage on teamwork, but waiting until this happens carries costs and risks.

It may be tempting to display moral indignation and to give a sermon on the importance of teamwork, but this is not likely to do much good. This reaction is likely to fall into a trap intended by SAM. Such a counter attack is likely to escalate the polarization and unwittingly provide SAM with an opening for more display, to stir up feelings and to recruit any partly alienated members.

Some of the complaints may have an element of truth and justification, even though the complaints and hostile attacks are overdrawn. An optimum leader may be able to spot truths in the criticism, and recognize them by acknowledgment and correction. This may to some extent disarm the attack. If one understands the deeper reasons for the rebel's attacks and feels some sympathy, it may be possible even to set up a kind of unobtrusive "side coalition" with SAM to work jointly on the problems both the leader and SAM see with the existing order of things.

On the other hand, if the rebellion is too obtrusive or if the level of unrest in the group against authority and the task is substantial, and any rebels begin to attract allies and become a serious threat in reality (not simply in the mode of symbolic theatrics) then the optimum leader may feel that it is necessary to mobilize all the support that he or she can muster, and act swiftly before the situation gets worse. If this is the last resort, the aim should be to disarm the opposition, or to remove the cause of unrest before it escalates further.

One danger in mobilizing support and making a direct attack, however, is that any direct attack is likely to recruit the support of any authoritarian members of the group who are already carrying on active opposition. The leader may appear to be "calling in the cops." Even an optimum leader, with substantial

Figure 11.6 *(continued)*

support, may unwittingly give the authoritarian elements in the
group more aid and comfort than he or she wishes, and may appear
to form a firm alliance with the authoritarians. This may later
turn out to be embarrassing and costly.

Remember also, that if one attacks with serious intent to carry
through, it is possible to lose, depending upon the number and
the power of seriously alienated members. An optimum approach
requires a careful estimate of the risks and possible costs
before "going for broke." Typically, it will not be possible to
have enough information to know just how much "on the fence" some
people in the group may be. The outcome may turn on a hair. One
should "count the votes" as accurately as possible, and then be
prepared for an unknown amount of fallout, or possible failure.

Source: From Robert F. Bales, "Bales Report," presented at the SYMLOG Users' Conference, San Diego, CA, September 1989. Reprinted by permission of SYMLOG Consulting Group.

Note: This report is based only on the ratings made by: PAT.

DIRECT OBSERVATION OF BEHAVIOR

The simplest way to do direct observation is to use the twenty-six-item
checklist to record the observer's judgment about the behavior of each
person in the team toward every other person after a period of team action,
or perhaps after each important phase of the action. This approach is
described by Bales in the *SYMLOG Case Study Kit* (1980). However, for a
more detailed analysis, each important act or image can be coded as it
occurs in the action or in some written description of the team activity. This
method, which is a more elaborate version of Bales's original twelve categories (Bales, 1950), is described in detail in the SYMLOG text (Bales &
Cohen, 1979. When one used the early Bales category system, every bit of
behavior that could elicit a response was scored; whereas, in the SYMLOG
version, only those acts or images are scored that stand out to the extent
that they might be remembered after the team activity is finished. This
simplifies the procedure when it comes to keeping up with fast-moving
dialogue. However, more complexity is introduced since the observer now
needs to consider activity at several different system levels.

The form suggested by Bales for recording SYMLOG messages is reproduced in Figure 11.7. Short definitions of the elements of the SYMLOG
message format are as follows:

Time: Two-digit number representing the minute from the beginning of the hour in
which the session occurs.

Who Acts: A short code name representing the name of the team member who is
making the communication and whose behavior is being observed.

Toward Whom: The other person (or the team as a whole) to whom the actor is
talking or toward whom the actor is acting.

ACT or NON: The classification of the communication at the behavioral level, either as ACT (an overt act toward the other intended to carry a communication content) or as NON (an unintentional nonverbal sign of emotion, feeling, or attitude).

Direction of ACT or NON: The directional classification in terms of the twenty-seven SYMLOG directions (including "AVE").

Ordinary Description of Behavior or Image: A few words in ordinary language indicating the content of the behavior or image.

PRO or CON: One of these two codes, or a question mark, is written to indicate whether the actor appears to be in favor of (PRO) or against (CON) the directional classification of the image selected for attention.

Direction of the Element of the Image: The directional classification that seems best to express the meaning the image has for the actor.

Image Level: A classification of the image according to one of the following six levels:

SEL: Images of the SELF of the actor as visualized by the actor.

OTH: OTHER team member, indicated by an abbreviation of the team member's name.

GRP: Images of the present team (GROUP).

SIT: Images of the SITUATION, the immediate environment.

SOC: Images of the SOCIETY in which the team exists.

FAN: Images that seem to arise out of the FANTASY of the actor, or to have a strong emotional meaning for the actor though based on actual experience.

On the back of the first form to be used, the observer draws a diagram showing the physical location of the various members of the team and indicates each of the members with a three-letter code. The location (or seating) chart will not only serve as a record of the persons present, but also help to understand the interaction process since location (or seating position) can have a marked effect on who speaks to whom.

In the first column on the left of the form in Figure 11.7, the time will be recorded if interaction is being coded as it takes place, especially if the observer wishes to check with a tape recording after the session or to compare notes with another observer. However, if the team is meeting for many occasions, it may be enough to record only the session at which the action takes place.

The next two columns record who is acting toward whom. If the person is talking to the team as a whole, the symbol "O" may be used, or perhaps "GRP." The next column is used to indicate whether the action is intended to communicate a message, even though it may not be made verbally. In this case it is coded as ACT. If the action is an unintentional nonverbal sign it is coded as NON. If an action has an intentional direction that is different from the unintentional nonverbal direction, two lines would be used to score the action.

Figure 11.7
The SYMLOG Interaction Scoring Form

Observer _____ Group_____ Date_____ Page_____

Draw a diagram of the physical location of group members on back of page 1

Time	Who Acts	Toward Whom	Act/ Non	Direc- tion	Ordinary Description of Behavior or Image	Pro/ Con	Direc- tion	Image Level

Source: Reprinted with permission of The Free Press, a Division of Macmillan, Inc., from *SYMLOG: A System for the Multiple Level Observation of Groups* by Robert F. Bales and Stephen P. Cohen with the assistance of Stephen A. Williamson, p. 411. Copyright © 1979 by The Free Press.

The next column is used to score the direction of the action in terms of the three dimensions. For example, an action that seemed managerial would be coded UF, or something that seemed funny as UB. Although Bales suggests that all twenty-seven possibilities be used as codes, the statements that are average (AVE) on all three dimensions are less likely to catch the observer's attention. The next wide column is for a few words to describe the behavior if there is no image included in the act, or the image if one is present.

The last three columns are used to record information about the image, where an image is defined as "a picture of an emotionally loaded focus of attention" (Bales & Cohen, 1979:167). If an image presented by one actor is picked up by others in a series of images, Bales refers to this as a "fantasy chain." The interest in an image may last for only a short period of time and then suddenly collapse. In the column labeled "Pro/Con" the observer records whether the actor seems to be in favor of the image (PRO) or against it (CON). Next the direction of the image is recorded, again in three dimensions. Finally, the image is coded according to one of the six levels. Images at the fantasy level are considered especially important since they are assumed to reveal basic values and preoccupations of the actor.

At the end of a session the codes for each individual can be summed to obtain an indication of the person's primary mode of interaction and the direction of the main images that were favored and those that were not. If enough observations are available, differences in patterns of interaction between each pair of actors in the team can be noted as well as between each actor and the team as a whole.

12
Combined Analysis: Conformity and Creativity in Negotiations

Social psychologists for the past ninety years have been wondering why people conform to group norms and how they could be creative in solving problems. The research that focuses on the issue of conformity includes the work of Sherif (1935), Asch (1955), Kelman (1958), Jahoda (1956), Milgram (1963), and Lifton (1961). The research that focuses on creative problem solving, especially through bargaining and negotiation includes the work of Follett (1924), Deutsch (1973), Fisher and Ury (1978), Burton (1979), and Pruitt (1983). The two streams of research actually complement each other, although few social psychologists study both, since to be creative one must be willing to break with existing norms to recombine or redefine old elements in new ways, or to provide some entirely new set of understandings about elements and relationships in a "paradigm shift."[1]

Most of the emphasis in research on creative problem solving has been placed on finding well-motivated and nonconforming individuals or establishing conditions in a group that facilitate a creative exchange rather than on the content of the creative act or on the level of creativity achieved. For example, McClelland (1961) suggests that the individual should be high on a need for achievement. Barron (1969) adds that in addition to being intelligent the person must be a nonconformist. Doob (1970) and Kelman and Cohen (1979) recommend the "problem-solving workshop" as a way of bringing people of diverse points of view together to find solutions to problems involving conflicts of interests.

If we wish to step back from our preoccupation with negotiations in relatively small groups and look with the anthropologists at larger units of

This paper was originally presented at a meeting of the *International Society of Political Psychology, Amsterdam, 1986.* Reprinted from *Israel Social Science Research*, 4, no. 2 (1986): 21-33.

society, we may conclude with Rosen (1984) that people are continually negotiating the social construction of reality in every sphere of life. All of these negotiations include both some commodity to be exchanged and some information about the relative position of the bargainers in society. That is, in small group terms, all social interaction has both task and social-emotional implications. However, many anthropologists and social psychologists, following Goffman (1959), have emphasized the social-emotional side of the "presentation of self in every day life" rather than the task side. Even so, the anthropologists remind us that if we wish to construct a category system to study conformity and creativity in negotiations, we would do well to make it general enough to cover other forms of social interaction, since all forms have essentially the same elements. On the other hand, our category system should not have so many categories that we have difficulty finding enough data to fill all the cells in our matrix, and it should be specific enough to reveal important aspects of negotiation. The roles persons play during this interaction are relatively constant and are fairly standardized, such as mediator or representative of one side, so our paradigm probably does not have to include a set of categories for roles. If we were observing fast-moving events involving large numbers of people in some form of collective behavior we might need some categories for role types.[2]

Since in the present instance our focus will be on international negotiations, with examples from negotiations between Israel and Egypt with third-party mediators, we will limit our concern to two of three types of activity that are carried out before, during, and after periods of international conflict. The classifications of the three types of activity are those used by the International Peace Academy (1978:16) and others to describe interventions by the United Nations and organizations with similar goals:

Peacekeeping: Third-party control of violence, often by interposition between two conflicting parties.

Peacemaking: An effort to settle a conflict through mediation, negotiation, or other peaceful forms.

Peacebuilding: Social change that seeks to eliminate the likelihood of direct or structural violence.

Five of the seven examples in the present study are of "peacemaking" with two references to "peacekeeping." The analysis of efforts toward "peacebuilding" involving everything from individual attitude change to changes in national and international structures will be left for another occasion.

CATEGORY SYSTEMS

Most category systems for the analysis of social interaction, as noted above, focus on the process of task and social-emotional behavior without regard to content (Hare, 1976:297-405). Bales's (1950) early system of twelve categories and more recent "SYMLOG" system for the multiple level analysis of behavior and images (Bales & Cohen, 1979) are two widely used examples.

A very early category system proposed by Carr (1929) recorded the topics discussed by number with an indication of agreement or disagreement after each topic was introduced. More recently Longabaugh (1963) and Hare and Mueller (1979) proposed systems that noted the content of discussion in terms of the four functional categories of Parsons (1961): adaptation, goal-attainment, integration, and pattern maintenance. They were concerned with the exchanges being made between discussants in terms of these four categories.

The most elaborate of the recent systems is that of Morley and Stephenson (1977). Their system, called Conference Process Analysis, was designed to study bargaining in labor-management relations. The system includes four categories for the "mode" of exchange: offer, accept, reject, and seek. There are nine categories for the content as a "resource," grouped under four headings: structural activity, outcome activity, acknowledgment, and other information. There are seven categories for the "referent," ranging from no referent to both parties. The unit of action is the simple sentence. Like Bales's early twelve IPA categories, every act is coded. In common with other systems of more than six categories, in any given situation most of the categories will appear with very low frequencies so that comparisons between situations are actually made on the basis of only a few of the categories. For example, Morley and Stephenson (1977:279) coded all the interaction in a three-session wage negotiation between representatives of labor and management. For the categories of "mode," 80 percent were classified as "offer" and 10 percent as "seek." For the categories of "resource," 30 percent suggested limits and 45 percent gave information. For the "referent," 45 percent were unclassified (since it was difficult to tell from a transcript who was being addressed) and 10 percent each were self, person, and other.

The problem of too many categories is not a major one since the system always can be collapsed to fit a particular occasion and it is better to have an initial system that is comprehensive and covers all of the space that is of theoretical or practical interest. In fact, Morley and Stephenson's system or the one that will be proposed below, even though it was developed with bargaining or negotiation in mind, is probably still too general to capture important aspects of the content of particular types of negotiation. Thus the user may need to add specific content categories for each new situation.

While Morley and Stephenson are concerned with the content and mode of the exchange, some category systems include both task content and social-emotional process categories. Stock and Thelen's (1958) system, based on the theory of Bion (1961), is an early example of the system that will be proposed below since it includes categories for the content of the work being done in terms of level of creativity and categories describing the social-emotional relationships between group members. Hare (1985a) and Hare and Naveh (1986) provide similar systems.

INTERACTION ANALYSIS

An example of the results of using the proposed scheme for Interaction Analysis (IA) is given in Table 12.1. The codes in the table are based on President Carter's account of his interaction with President Sadat at Camp David in 1978 (Carter, 1982). These will be analyzed and compared with the interaction between President Carter and Prime Minister Begin later in the paper. The table includes twenty cells for each of the participants in a dyadic exchange. In a larger group, especially when it is not clear who is speaking to whom, it will be enough to include twenty cells for the acts each person initiates and twenty cells for acts each person receives. Reading the table from left to right, the first ten cells represent the content of task contributions. The five rows represent the five levels of creativity identified by Taylor (1975) and adapted for content analysis by Hare (1982, 1985a) and Hare and Naveh (1985). In brief, contributions at the C1 level either provide background facts or ways of avoiding a problem rather than finding a solution. The C2 level includes suggestions for methods of improved communication or increasing the skills of the particpants. The C3 level includes suggestions for combinations of the interests of the participants in "package deals." The C4 level provides new perspectives on a problem by extending old concepts to fit new situations. The highest C5 level provides new understanding of both forms and relationships, including ideas that give a new definition of the situation as well as those that constitute a "paradigm shift."

Table 12.1
Summary of Interaction Analysis Scores for Carter to Sadat and Sadat to Carter in Terms of Creativity and Pressures toward Conformity, Camp David, 1978

Carter to Sadat						Sadat to Carter					
Creat Level	Task		Con Cat	Social-emotional		Creat Level	Task		Con Cat	Social-emotional	
	+	−		+	−		+	−		+	−
5	0	0	Img	8UPF	4UNB	5	1o	0	Img	1UPF	2N
4	0	0	C-A	0	0	4	0	0	C-A	1	0
3	10o 1a	0	P-N	3	1	3	2o 4a	3r	P-N	2	0
2	9o 1a	1r	D-U	0	3	2	3o 8a	1r	D-U	0	0
1	1o 2s	0	S-E	4	0	1	4o 1a 1s	0	S-E	0	0

The two columns in the task area are for positive and negative contributions. If the primary purpose of a contribution is to provide new material, then the contribution is coded in the positive column. However, if the primary purpose is to contradict or attack an existing idea, then the contribution is coded in the negative column. In addition to coding the level of creativity, positive contributions are coded according to one of the three exchange categories: accepts, seeks, or offers. The negative contributions also are coded according to one of the three exchange categories: rejects, deprives, or ignores.

The social-emotional categories again provide two columns for positive and negative acts and five rows for types of acts, arranged, as were the categories for creativity, in a "cybernetic hierarchy," from low at the bottom of the table to high at the top. The four dimensions of behavior are those previously described by Hare (1972, 1976, 1982, 1985b). The two bottom categories in the social-emotional columns represent the two ends of the dimension Serious versus Expressive, where expressive means joking, laughing, and other forms of relief from the task. The two categories above represent the ends of the dimension Downward versus Upward, where downward is submissive behavior and upward is dominant behavior. The next set of categories are Positive versus Negative, or friendly versus unfriendly. The fourth set of behavior categories are Conforming (to existing norms) versus Anticonforming. The top set of categories are for Images. Images are emotionally loaded word pictures used by the actors in their attempts to persuade each other. The definition of an image and the method of coding them according to different levels of referents are those proposed by Bales (Bales & Cohen, 1979).

In his SYMLOG system Bales uses three dimensions for coding both behavior and images. In the present system, four dimensions are used. The Upward-Downward and Positive-Negative dimensions are the same as those of Bales. Bales's third dimension, Forward-Backward, has been split into two components, Serious-Expressive and Conforming-Anticonforming. In Bales's system Forward behavior is both serious and conforming while backward behavior is both expressive and anticonforming. In many situations the three dimensions of Bales are enough to capture the variance one is concerned about. However, on those occasions where some of the serious persons are also anticonforming and some of the expressive persons are also conforming, the four dimensions for both behavior and images can provide a better fit with the data.

The images that the actor is in favor of (PRO) are coded in the positive column. The images that the actor does not favor (CON) are coded in the negative column. Although Bales's system distinguishes six levels of images, for most purposes it is enough to find the modal image by summing over all levels, as an indication of the location in the four- (or three-) dimensional space that the actor favors or does not favor. The categories for images are placed at the top of the social-emotional columns, in a position comparable to the fifth level of creativity, since they tend to represent definitions of the situation that the actor wishes others to accept or reject.

The cybernetic hierarchy for the categories of behavior in each social-emotional column is presumed to work in the following way. The minimum positive reinforcement can be given to persons by taking them seriously and the minimum negative reinforcement by taking their suggestions as a joke. A more positive reinforcement would be to act submissively and seek directions from the other and a negative reinforcement to act in a dominating fashion. An even more effective positive reinforcement would be to be friendly or for negative reinforcement to be unfriendly. At the top of the hierarchy of positive behavioral reinforcements would be to conform to existing norms governing a relationship or to endorse the norms. For a negative reinforcement one would act in a nonconforming way. The modes of exchange used in connection with the task categories are presumed to provide pressure in a similar way. On the positive side, the order from low to high, would be: offers, seeks, and accepts. On the negative side the order would be: ignores, deprives, and rejects.

As noted earlier, most category systems, including this one, have more categories than one can use with a given set of data. Sometimes one may be coding the minutes of meetings or other documents that do not reveal the process. A record of negotiation may have only the proposals of each side and the final outcome but no indication of the actual bargaining behavior. On other occasions there may be little indication of content, only sets of adjectives describing the behavior of the participants, as on a SYMLOG questionnaire. Thus one may sometimes use only the task categories and on other occasions only the social-emotional categories. Also for many types of negotiation the participants seldom seem to go above creativity Level 3 of "package deals." As a further simplification in the use of the category system, one does not need to code every sentence, but rather, following the practice suggested by Bales for SYMLOG, code only those acts whose content or form seems especially important and which are of the sort likely to be remembered by the participants after the meeting.

EXAMPLES OF CREATIVITY IN NEGOTIAITON

Although many discussions of negotiation and mediation mention methods or strategies for achieving success, few describe them in terms of creativity. An exception is the article by Fogg (1985) entitled "Dealing with conflict: A repertoire of creative, peaceful approaches." He lists many possible approaches according to who, what, where, when, how, and why of negotiation. Some of the examples from Fogg's list illustrate the content of the five levels of creativity:

C5—persuasion to or acceptance of new, integrative values (p. 355).

C4—"coupling" by giving a new meaning of signal added to a diplomatic action to facilitate communication (p. 255).

C3—package deals (p. 340).

C2—Osgood's graduated reciprocation in tension reduction (p. 334), Fisher's fractionating conflict (p. 339), Burton's controlled communication, Doob's workshop, and Kelman and Cohen's problem-solving workshop (p. 350).

C1—identification and ignoring of intractable issues (p. 344).

Similar lists that provide examples of categories C1 throuch C3 can be found in books or articles by Walton (1969), Scher (1974), Gulliver (1979), the International Labour Office (1980), Wall (1981), Fisher (1983), and Kolb (1983). Pruitt (1983:36) recognizes the importance of decisions at higher levels of creativity in his observation that "integrative agreements are likely to be more stable. Compromises are often unsatisfactory to one or both parties, causing the issue to come up again at a later time."

NEGOTIATIONS INVOLVING EGYPT AND ISRAEL

The third-party mediations involving Egypt and Israel that have been analyzed using the Interaction Analysis categories include Bernadotte's 1948 attempts to establish a cease-fire and gain recogniton from the Arab states for the new state of Israel, Jackson's mid-1955 attempts to facilitate communication between Egypt and Israel, Anderson's similar mission in 1955-56, Kissinger's shuttle diplomacy in 1973, and President Carter's interventions at Camp David in 1978 leading to a peace treaty.[3]

There are also two accounts of the activities of chiefs of staff of the United Nations Truce-Supervision Organization. One account is by Burns who served from 1954 through 1957 and the other by Bull who served from 1963 through 1970.

The accounts, by the mediator or by one of the parties in the mediation, vary considerably in the amount of detail recorded, especially in the social-emotional area. Since President Carter provides the most complete record of his negotiations with President Sadat and Prime Minister Begin at Camp David, this instance of mediation will be described first in some detail, for comparison later with the other case studies.

CARTER, SADAT, AND BEGIN AT CAMP DAVID, 1978

Several of the participants in the negotiations at Camp David in 1978 have published their accounts of the process. For the present purpose, the account of President Carter of the United States (1982) gives the most detailed record of his discussions with President Sadat of Egypt and Prime Minister Begin of Israel. Although Carter had hoped the leaders of the two nations might be able to sit together in his study and resolve their differences while he took notes, his plan for "keeping faith" in this way could not be realized. Both Sadat and Begin were inclined to defend their own positions rather than seek common "non-zero-sum" solutions. After the third day of the discussions Carter met Sadat and Begin separately. All three did not come together again until the final ceremony at the White House in Washington, D.C., to sign the peace agreements. Although as in most international negotiations, much of the work of seeking points of agreement and drafting proposals was done by staff members who seldom appeared in the headlines, for the present analysis we will focus only on the principal negotiators.

The numbers in Tables 12.1 and 12.2 represent summaries of scores for Sadat and Carter and Begin and Carter. Even though all three were present in the same room during the first few joint meetings, very little of the interaction between Sadat and Begin is recorded in detail, other than to note that they were arguing with each other and the issues that concerned them, so that there is no table summarizing the interaction between Sadat and Begin. However, the main reason for not including their interaction is that the focus of this research is on the methods used by the mediator to persuade the representatives of the two sides. All of the other six cases of mediation between Israel and Egypt, to be discussed here, involved a version of "shuttle diplomacy." With the exception of some occasions when the chiefs of staff for the UN Truce Supervision Organization were able to meet lower ranking military commanders from both sides, the mediators usually were able to meet only separately with the representatives of one side at a time.

Table 12.2
Summary of Interaction Analysis Scores for Carter to Begin and Begin to Carter in Terms of Creativity and Pressures toward Conformity, Camp David, 1978

Carter to Begin						Begin to Carter					
Creat Level	Task +	−	Con Cat	Social-emotional +	−	Creat Level	Task +	−	Con Cat	Social-emotional +	−
5	1o	1r	Img	11UPF	5UNF	5	1o	0	Img	0	0
4	1a	0	C-A	0	0	4	1o	0	C-A	1	1
3	5o	3r	P-N	3	7	3	5o 2a	4r	P-N	0	4
2	9o 1a	1r	D-U	0	9	2	7o 5a 1s	2r	D-U	0	2
1	2o 1s	1r	S-E	10	1	1	7o	0	S-E	3	2

Reading Table 12.1 from left to right we see that Carter's task behavior with Sadat consisted mainly of offering ideas at creativity levels 2 and 3. An example of C2 is when Carter offered Sadat the procedural suggestion that "once a framework for peace was signed, aides could draft a peace treaty over a period of not more than three months" (Carter, 1982:339). To this Sadat agreed, giving him one entry as an agreement at the C2 level. Carter's suggestion to Sadat that "sovereignty issues are different in the Sinai and Golan Heights from the West Bank. Begin cannot now accept sovereignty over the West Bank, and I agree with him. For the time being we must permit Jews and Arabs to live together. We should be able to work out something on self rule . . . " (1982:361) was part of a statement about a "package" that he thought could be acceptable to both sides, and was coded as an offer at the C3 level. Carter accepted, sought, or rejected only a few of Sadat's offerings in the task area.

In the social-emotional area we see that Carter's interaction with Sadat was mainly serious, upward (dominant), and positive. Although Carter used a variety of images at different levels in his attempt to persuade both Sadat and Begin to get along together, Tables 12.1 and 12.2 show only the summary of images directed to either Sadat or Begin with an indication of the typical content. Carter tried to reinforce an image of Upward-Positive-Forward behavior with Sadat and discourage an image of Upward-Negative-Backward behavior, that is, of one who was too critical and not cooperating with the task. With Begin, Carter tried to discourage his Upward-Negative-Forward behavior.

Sadat's task behavior with Carter was characterized by offers of background facts (C1) and agreement with Carter's suggestions at Levels C2 and C3. Very few instances of behavior or images were recorded in the social-emotional area; however, Carter found him much friendlier and easier to get on with than Begin.

In Table 12.2 we see that in the task area Carter mainly offered Begin suggestions at the C2 level. He rejected some of Begin's suggestions. The suggestions offered and rejected at the C5 level for Carter and Begin both occurred during the first few minutes of discussion when Begin arrived at Camp David. From Begin's remarks Carter concluded that Begin was clearly planning for an agreement at Camp David only on general principles, with the details left for their ministers to negotiate. This was coded as Begin to Carter offers C5, since this proposition of Begin's involved the whole "definition of the situation" for the activity at Camp David. Carter records: "I objected strongly to this plan, and told the Prime Minister that we three principals could not expect others to settle major issues later if we could not do so now, and that all the controversial questions should be addressed by us directly" (Carter, 1982:330). This was coded as Carter to Begin rejects C5 and Carter to Begin offers C5.

The exchange between Carter and Begin coded as an offer of C4 by Begin and an acceptance by Carter might have been the other way round. The text is not clear, so I gave Begin the benefit of the doubt. The incident occurred on the twelfth day while Carter was having a discussion with Begin and his aides, still trying to find some formula by which Begin would agree to sign the peace proposals. Carter records that he thought the discussion would never end since Begin was obviously pained and was shouting words like "ultimatum," "excessive demands," and "political suicide." "However he finally promised to submit to the Knesset within two weeks the question: 'If agreement is reached on all other Sinai issues, will the settlers be withdrawn?' I believed this concession would be enough for Sadat. Breakthrough!" (Carter, 1982:396). This was coded as Begin to Carter offers C4 and Carter to Begin accepts C4, although Begin may have "finally promised" only at the urging of Carter. In any event, the suggestion is coded as C4 since it involved a redefinition of the roles of Begin and the Knesset.

Compared with Sadat, in the task area, Begin offered Carter more suggestions, however Carter was more rejecting than accepting of Begin's ideas. Begin in his turn was slightly more rejecting and less accepting of Carter's suggestions than Sadat. In the social-emotional area Begin tended to be negative. Although it does not show in the tables, Carter imposed pressure toward conformity through his direct behavior when both Sadat and Begin were present. In contrast Carter tended to use images as a method of influence when he was alone with one of the participants.

VARIATIONS ON THE MEDIATION THEME

Of the various efforts toward mediation included as case material for this study, Kissinger's "shuttle" between Egypt and Israel in 1973 is most similar to that of Carter's mediation at Camp David (Kissinger, 1982). Sadat was representing the Egyptians in both cases, Kissinger also had high status as secretary of state for the United States, and the issue was to negotiate a peace agreement. However, Kissinger did not meet Sadat and Golda Meir, then prime minister of Israel, around the same table.

In the task area Sadat opened the discussion with statements of his definition of the situation (offers coded as C4 and C5). However, Sadat's initial statement would have been so unacceptable to the Israelis that Kissinger decided to change the subject rather than attempt to respond. Later Kissinger made his own proposals to Sadat, at various levels. Sadat accepted enough of these so that Kissinger felt he had a basis for negotiation with Israel. Sadat was friendly to Kissinger. Meir did not make any suggestions to Kissinger nor did she seem to have accepted any of his suggestions. Much of her interaction consisted of negative reactions to the way she felt Israel was being treated. Both Sadat and Meir gave negative images of their own countries as being Downward, in a weak power position.

In terms of level-of-task demands, Bernadotte also faced a difficult situation since he had to negotiate a cease-fire between Israel and the surrounding Arab states when they were not yet ready to accept the legitimacy of the new state of Israel (Bernadotte, 1951; Ben-Gurion, 1972). Berna-dotte's experience with the Egyptian side was similar to that of Kissinger and Carter some years later. The Egyptians were warm and friendly but their initial statements of what was possible, in this case that no Arab state was prepared to recognize an independent Israel, seemed to leave no room for maneuver. However, Bernadotte was not dismayed and kept pressing for more information until he felt he had found some opening for negotiation. Much of Bernadotte's task behavior with both sides consisted of giving facts about the situation as he saw it (C1) and suggesting "packages" that he thought might be acceptable to both sides (C3), most of which were rejected immediately by the Israelis. Although Bernadotte seemed to be making some progress he was assassinated by members of an Israeli paramilitary group before his negotiations could come to fruition.

The mediation efforts of Jackson in 1955 (Jackson, 1983) and Anderson in 1956 (Ben-Gurion, 1972) are similar in that both were providing "good offices" as they shuttled between Cairo and Jerusalem in an effort to promote face-to-face talks between representatives of the two countries. Much of the discussion involved procedural matters (C2).

Both Burns (1969) and Bull (1976) wrote their own accounts of their activities as chiefs of staff of the United Nations Truce Supervision Organization. As with Bernadotte, their problems were not limited to those on the Egyptian border. Both were concerned primarily with establishing the facts when border incidents occurred and renegotiating the cease-fire agreements.

DISCUSSION

There are two main advantages of using a comprehensive category system. One is that it becomes possible to compare various forms of interaction in terms of the categories. The other is that, regardless of the effectiveness of the category system, the close line by line analysis of the text may reveal important aspects of the situation that would not be apparent from a less concentrated reading. In terms of the present categories for Interaction Analysis we see that each of the mediating tasks in this series required a particular level of creativity for its solution and the mediators seldom exceeded this upper level. All of the tasks required the gathering and exchanging of facts (C1). However, the tasks of maintaining a cease-fire and of providing "good offices" between parties mainly required suggestions that would facilitate communication or provide a better assessment of the facts, all at the C2 level. Only occasionally was it necessary to suggest some type of exchange in the form of a "package." The tasks of peace-making mediated by Bernadotte, Kissinger, and Carter not only required elaborating older ideas to fit the present situation (C4), but also, on occasion, completely redefining the situation for one or more of the actors (C5). In addition the mediators had to be sensitive to issues that could not be resolved. To allow the negotiations to continue, the mediators had to find ways of avoiding these issues, obscuring them in ambiguous wording, or using other devices that left the problem unsolved (C1). On the social-emotional side, most of the negotiations began in a friendly or neutral manner with an emphasis on the task, but as the participants warmed up, and especially if the negotiations were not going in their favor, they tended to become more negative and introduce emotional images of themselves and the other side.

It is evident that a third party can play a part at a distance from the adversaries or over an extended period of time. But it is better if all parties are in the same room or area, as with Carter, or can travel rapidly between parties, as with Jackson. With face-to-face or rapid communication there is the possibility of immediately overcoming blocks that one side or the other has thrown up before they have a chance to cause a serious disruption in the negotiations.

Some of the cultural differences between Egyptians and Israelis are evident as continuing themes through these negotiations, perhaps enhanced by the fact that all of the mediators were either from the United States or Europe. The traditional warmth and hospitality of the Arabs was responded to positively by the mediators, although they did not always realize that it would be better to avoid dealing directly with the conditions set out in their opening statements, that were intended primarily for public consumption. On the other hand the mediators were continually put off by the negative, interruptng style of argument used by the Israelis. Several of them noted that it was only after they had attended a session of the Israeli Knesset that they realized that most Israeli politicians seemed to behave in the same way.

Although not covered by the category system, at least not when one focuses on the three or more principal persons involved in the negotiation, it is obvious that international negotiations involve many actors from staff assistants through representatives of other countries who have an interest in the issue. For example, Bernadotte would have had a different set of problems had not England been supporting the Arab side. Carter could not have found a solution to the removal of the Israeli airfields in the Sinai without the resources of the United States to build new ones. Without the support of Russia and Czechoslovakia, Egypt would not have been able to prepare for war or reequip its losses. Without support from France and the United States, Israel would have had no modern fighter planes for defense or attack. Kissinger was perhaps the most concerned about the relationships between the various countries as his Middle East shuttle took him to Moscow and other important capitals. In every case the Arab countries were all too aware of the opinions of their neighboring Arab states and the problems they would face if they seemed to be too friendly with Israel. For all this complexity the mediator still plays a crucial role in facilitating both the problem solving and the interpersonal relations among the participants, but time and time again negotiations come to a halt because of factors that lie outside the mediator's control.

NOTES

1. See Hare, 1982:90-100 and 1983b:9-11 for brief summaries of research on these two themes.

2. See, for example, the dramaturgical categories of Hare (1985b).

3. See Touval (1982) for an introduction to these mediations and others during the same period.

References

Adair-Heeley, Charlene B., & Garwood, R. Dave. (1989). Helping teams be the best they can be: The message in the milk bottle. *Production & Inventory Management Review & APICS News*, *9*(7), 22-25.

Adams, John. (1988). The role of the creative outlook on team building. In W. Brendan Reddy with Kaleel Jamison (Eds.), *Team building*, pp. 98-106. Alexandria, VA: NTL Institute for Applied Behavioral Science. San Diego: University Associates.

Allen, K. Eileen, Holm, Vanja A., & Schiefelbusch, Richard L. (Eds.). (1978). *Early intervention: A team approach*. Baltimore: University Park Press.

Asch, Solomon E. (1955). Opinions and social pressure. *Scientific American*, *193*(5), 31-35.

Azar, Edward E. (1985). Protracted international conflicts: Ten proposals. *International Interactions*, *12*(1), 59-70.

Bachman, Wallace. (1988). Nice guys finish first: A SYMLOG analysis of U.S. Naval Commands. In Richard B. Polley, A. Paul Hare, & Philip J. Stone (Eds.), *The SYMLOG practitioner*, pp. 133-153. New York: Praeger.

Bales, Robert F. (1950). *Interaction process analysis: A method for the study of small groups*. Cambridge, MA: Addison-Wesley.

_____. (1954). In conference. *Harvard Business Review*, *32*, 44-50.

_____. (1970). *Personality and interpersonal behavior*. New York: Holt, Rinehart & Winston.

_____. (1980). *SYMLOG case study kit: With instructions for a group self study*. New York: Free Press.

_____. (1988). Overview of the SYMLOG system: Measuring and changing behavior in groups. San Diego: SYMLOG Consulting Group.

Bales, Robert F., & Cohen, Stephen P., with Williamson, Stephen A. (1979). *SYMLOG: A system for the multiple level observation of groups*. New York: Free Press.

Bales, Robert F., & Hare, A. Paul. (1965). The diagnostic use of the interaction profile. *Journal of Social Psychology*, *67*, 239-258.

Barkman, Donald F. (1987). Team discipline: Put performance on the line. *Personnel Journal*, *66*(3), 58-63.

Barron, Frank. (1969). *Creative person and creative process.* New York: Holt, Rinehart & Winston.

Bassin, Mark. (1988). Teamwork at General Foods: New & improved. *Personnel Journal, 67*(5), 62-70.

Beckhard, Richard. (1966). An organization improvement program in a decentralized organization. *Journal of Applied Behavioral Science, 2*(1), 3-25.

Beer, Jennifer E. (1986). *Peacemaking in your neighborhood: Reflections on an experiment in community mediation.* Philadelphia: New Society Publishers.

Beer, Michael. (1976). The technology of organization development. In Marvin Dunnette (Ed.), *Handbook of industrial and organizational psychology*, pp. 937-993. Chicago: Rand McNally.

Belzer, Ellen J. (1989). Twelve ways to better team building. *Working Woman, 14*(8), 12, 14.

Ben-Gurion, David. (1972). *Israel: A personal history.* Tel Aviv: Sabra Books.

Bennis, Warren G., & Shepard, Herbert A. (1956). A theory of group development. *Human Relations, 9*, 415-437.

Berger, Florence, & Vanger, Rachel. (1986). Building your hospitality team. *Cornell Hotel & Restaurant Administration Quarterly, 26*(4), 82-90.

Bernadotte, Folke. (1951). *To Jerusalem.* London: Hodder & Stoughton.

Bion, W. R. (1961). *Experiences in groups.* New York: Basic Books.

Blake, Robert R., & Mouton, Jane Srygley. (1968). *Corporate excellence through Grid organization development.* Houston: Gulf Publishing.

_____. (1976). *Consultation.* Reading, MA: Addison-Wesley.

_____. (1984). *Solving costly organizational conflicts.* San Francisco: Jossey-Bass.

_____. (1985). *The Managerial Grid III.* Houston: Gulf Publishing.

Blake, Robert F., Mouton, Jane Srygley, Barnes, Louis B., & Greiner, Larry E. (1964). Breakthrough in organization development. *Harvard Business Review, 42*(6), 133-138.

Blake, Robert F., Mouton, Jane Srygley, & McCanse, Anne Adams. (1989). *Change by design.* Reading, MA: Addison-Wesley.

Blake, Robert F., Mouton, Jane Srygley, & Williams, Martha Shipe. (1981). *The academic administrator grid: A guide to developing effective management teams.* San Francisco: Jossey-Bass.

Blau, Peter M. (1964). *Exchange of power in social life.* New York: Wiley.

Blechert, Toné F., Christiansen, Marianne F., & Kari, Nancy. (1987). Intraprofessional team building. *American Journal of Occupational Therapy, 41*(9), 576-582.

Blumberg, Herbert H. (1992). Bargaining. In A. Paul Hare et al., *Small Group research: A handbook.* Norwood, NJ: ABLEX.

Bocialetti, Gene. (1988). Teams and the management of emotion. In W. Brendan Reddy with Kaleel Jamison (Eds.), *Team building*, pp. 62-71. Alexandria, VA: NTL Institute for Applied Behavioral Science. San Diego: University Associates.

Boss, R. Wayne, & McConkie, Mark L. (1981). The destructive impact of a positive team-building intervention. *Group and Organization Studies, 6*(1), 45-56.

Brandstatter, Hermann, Davis, James H., & Stocker-Kreichgauer, Gisela (Eds.). (1982). *Group decision making.* London: Academic Press.

Broadwell, Laura. (1987). Business games: They're more than child's play. *Successful Meetings, 36*(7), 36-39.

_____. (1989). Howdy, trail riders: How about meeting at a dude ranch? *Successful Meetings*, *38*(1), 31-33.

Brown, Nancy J. (1988). Do you have ROCS in your head? The illusions of rationality, objectivity, consciousness, and separability in team building. In W. Brendan Reddy with Kaleel Jamison (Eds.), *Team building*, pp. 72-75. Alexandria, VA: NTL Institute for Applied Behavioral Science. San Diego: University Associates.

Bruce, Nigel. (1980). *Teamwork for preventive care*. Chichester, UK: Research Studies Press.

Buhler, Pat M., & McCann, Michael. (1989). Building your management teams: Part I. *Supervision*, *50*(9), 14-15, 26.

Bull, Odd. (1976). *War and peace in the Middle East*. London: Cooper.

Buller, Paul F. (1986). The team building-task performance relation: Some conceptual and methodological refinements. *Group & Organization Studies*, *11*(3), 147-168.

Burke, Kenneth. (1968). Dramatism. In David L. Sills (Ed.), *International encyclopedia of the social sciences*, pp. 445-452. New York: Macmillan.

Burke, W. Warner. (1988). Team building. In W. Brendan Reddy with Kaleel Jamison (Eds.), *Team building*, pp. 3-14. Alexandria, VA: NTL Institute for Applied Behavioral Sciences. San Diego: University Associates.

Burns, E.L.M. (1969). *Between Arab and Israeli*. Beirut: Institute for Palestine Studies.

Burton, John W. (1979). *Deviance, terrorism, and war*. Oxford: Martin Robinson.

_____. (1985). The history of international conflict resolution. *International Interactions*, *12*(1), 45-57.

Byrd, Richard E. (1988). How to stay in charge—even with a consultant. In W. Brendan Reddy with Kaleel Jamison (Eds.), *Team building*, pp. 150-160. Alexandria, VA: NTL Institute for Applied Behavioral Science. San Diego: University Associates.

Carr, Lowell J. (1929). Experimental sociology: A preliminary note on theory and method. *Social Forces*, *8*, 63-74.

Carter, Jimmy. (1982). *Keeping faith*. New York: Bantam Books.

Cartwright, Dorwin, & Zander, Alvin (Eds.). (1968). *Group dynamics: Research and theory*. New York: Harper & Row.

Casey, David. (1985). When is a team not a team? *Personnel Management*, *17*(1), 26-29.

Chance, Paul. (1989). Great experiments in team chemistry. *Across the Board*, *26*(5), 18-25.

Chubin, Daryl E., Porter, Alan L., Rossini, Frederick A., & Connolly, Terry (Eds.). (1986). *Interdisciplinary analysis and research: Theory and practice of problem-focused research and development*. Mt. Airy, MD: Lomond Publications.

Colantvono, Susan L., & Schnidman, Ava A. (1988). E pluribus unum: Building multifunctional work teams. In W. Brendan Reddy with Kaleel Jamison (Eds.), *Team building*, pp. 187-191. Alexandria, VA: NTL Institute for Applied Behavioral Science. San Diego: University Associates.

Conlin, Joseph. (1989). Forging team power. *Successful Meetings*, *38*(1), 26-29.

Conlon, Edward J., & Barr, Steven H. (1989). A framework for understanding group feedback. *Advances in Group Processes*, *6*, 27-48.

Cook, Karen S. (Ed.). (1987). *Social exchange theory*. Beverly Hills, CA: Sage.

Dannemiller, Kathleen D. (1988). Team building at a macro level, or "Ben Gay" for arthritic organizations. In W. Brendan Reddy with Kaleel Jamison (Eds.), *Team building*, pp. 107-115. Alexandria, VA: NTL Institute for Applied Behavioral Science. San Diego: University Associates.

Davidson, Jeffrey P. (1984). Teaming up to solve problems. *Today's Office, 19*(7), 25-26.

_____. (1985). A task-focused approach to team building. *Personnel, 62*(3), 16-18.

Davis, James H., Hornik, John, & Hornseth, John P. (1970). Group decision schemes and strategy preferences in a sequential response task. *Journal of Personality and Social Psychology, 15*(4), 397-408.

Davis, James H., & Stasson, Mark F. (1988). Small group performance: Past and present research trends. *Advances in Group Processes, 5*, 245-277.

Desai, Narayan. (1972). *Towards nonviolent revolution*. Rajghat, Varanasi, India: Sarva Seva Sangh Prakashan.

Deutsch, Morton. (1973). *The resolution of conflict*. New Haven, CT: Yale University Press.

Diehl, Michael, & Stroebe, Wolfgang. (1987). Productivity loss in brainstorming groups: Toward the solution of a riddle. *Journal of Personality and Social Psychology, 53*, 497-509.

Doob, Leonard W. (Ed.). (1970). *Resolving conflict in Africa*. New Haven, CT: Yale University Press.

Drexler, Allan B., Sibbet, David, & Forrester, Russell H. (1988). The team performance model. In W. Brendan Reddy with Kaleel Jamison (Eds.), *Team building*, pp. 45-61. Alexandria, VA: NTL Institute for Applied Behavioral Science. San Diego: University Associates.

Dyer, William G. (1987). *Team building: Issues and alternatives* (2nd ed.). Reading, MA: Addison-Wesley.

Eden, Dov. (1985). Team development: A true field experiment employing three levels of rigor. *Journal of Applied Psychology, 70*(1), 94-100.

Effrat, Andrew. (1968). Editor's introduction [Applications of Parsonian theory]. *Sociological Inquiry, 38*(Spring), 97-103.

_____. (1976). Introduction [Social change and development]. In Jan J. Loubser, Rainer C. Baum, Andrew Effrat, & Victor M. Lidz (Eds.), *Explorations in general theory in social science*, pp. 662-680. New York: Free Press.

Eisenhardt, Kathleen M. (1989). Making fast strategic decisions in high-velocity environments. *Academy of Management Journal, 32*(3), 543-576.

Emerson, Richard M. (1976). Social exchange theory. *Annual Review of Sociology, 2*, 335-362.

Fiorelli, Joseph S. (1988). Power in work groups: Team member's perspectives. *Human Relations, 41*(1), 1-12.

Fisher, Ronald J. (1983). Third party consultation as a method of intergroup conflict resolution: A review of studies. *Journal of Conflict Resolution, 27*(2), 301-334.

_____. (1987). Pre-negotiation problem solving discussions in protracted conflict. Saskatoon & Regina, Sask., Can.: University of Saskatoon, Canadian Institute for International Affairs.

Fisher, Roger, & Ury, William. (1978). *International mediation*. New York: International Peace Academy.

Foa, Edna B., & Foa, Uriel G. (1980). Resource theory: Interpersonal behavior as exchange. In Kenneth J. Gergen, Martin S. Greenberg, & Richard H. Willis (Eds.), *Social exchange*, pp. 77-94. New York: Plenum.

Foa, Uriel, & Foa, Edna B. (1974). *Societal structures of the mind.* Springfield, IL: Charles C. Thomas.

Foddy, Margaret. (1989). Information control as a bargaining tactic in social exchange. *Advances in Group Processes, 6,* 139-178.

Fogg, Richard W. (1985). Dealing with conflict: A repertoire of creative peaceful approaches. *Journal of Conflict Resolution, 29*(2), 330-358.

Follett, Mary P. (1924). *Creative experience.* New York: Longmans, Green.

Foushee, H. Clayton. (1984). Dyads and triads at 35,000 feet: Factors affecting group process and aircrew performance. *American Psychologist, 39,* 885-893.

Frame, Robert M., Hess, Randy K., & Nielsen, Warren R. (1982). *The OD source book: A practitioner's guide.* San Diego: University Associates.

Francis, Dave, & Young, Don. (1979). *Improving work groups: A practical manual for team building.* San Diego: University Associates.

Friedlander, Frank. (1966). Performance and interactional dimensions of organizational work groups. *Journal of Applied Psychology, 50*(3), 257-265.

Friedlander, Frank, & Green, P. Toni. (1977). Life styles and conflict-coping structures. *Group and Organization Studies, 2,* 101-112.

Gadon, Herman. (1988). The newcomer and the ongoing work group. In W. Brendan Reddy with Kaleel Jamison (Eds.), *Team building*, pp. 161-175. Alexandria, VA: NTL Institute for Applied Behavioral Science. San Diego: University Associates.

Geber, Beverly. (1989). A global approach to training. *Training, 26*(9), 42-47.

Genovés, Santiago. (1979). *The Acali experiment: Six women and five men on a raft across the Atlantic.* New York: Times Books.

George, Paul S. (1987). Team building without tears. *Personnel Journal, 66*(11), 122-129.

George, William W. (1977). Task teams for rapid growth. *Harvard Business Review, 55*(2), 71-80.

Gergen, Kenneth J., Greenberg, Martin S., & Willis, Richard H. (Eds.). (1980). *Social exchange: Advances in theory and research.* New York: Plenum.

Gersick, Connie J. G. (1988). Time and transition in work teams: Toward a new model of group development. *Academy of Management Journal, 1*(1), 9-41.

Goffman, Erving. (1959). *The presentation of self in everyday life.* Garden City, NY: Doubleday.

_____. (1974). *Frame analysis: An essay on the organization of experience.* New York: Harper & Row.

Golembiewski, Robert T. (1988). Working with teams in the public and business sectors: Ways of dealing with major differences. In W. Brendan Reddy with Kaleel Jamison (Eds.), *Team building*, pp. 124-133. Alexandria, VA: NTL Institute for Applied Behavioral Science. San Diego: University Associates.

Golin, Anne, & Ducanis, Alex J. (1981). *The interdisciplinary team: A handbook for the education of exceptional children.* Rockville, MD: Aspen Systems Corporation.

Gordon, Jack, & Zemke, Ron. (1986). Making them more creative. *Training, 23*(5), 30-45.

Gordon, William J. J. (1961). *Synectics: The development of creative capacity.* New York: Collier Books.

Gray, James. (1986). Team building: Transforming individuals into work groups. *Credit Union Executive, 26*(4), 24-25.

Greenberg, Jeanne, & Greenberg, Herb. (1988). Developing a winning team. *Agency Sales Magazine, 18*(7), 56-60.

Guilford, Joy P. (1975). Creativity: A quarter century of progress. In Irving A. Taylor and Jacob W. Getzels (Eds.), *Perspectives in creativity*, pp. 37-59. Chicago: Aldine.

Gulliver, P. H. (1979). *Disputes and negotiations.* New York: Academic Press.

Hackman, J. Richard, & Oldham, Greg R. (1980). *Work design.* Reading, MA: Addison-Wesley.

Hagen, Robert P. (1985). Team building. *Manage, 37*(1), 26-28.

Hall, Jim. (1985). Productivity improvement through team building and organizational redevelopment: Evaluating the experiences of a human services agency at the county level. *Public Personnel Management, 14*(4), 409-416.

Hallstein, Richard W. (1989). Team un-building. *Training & Development Journal, 43*(6), 56-58.

Hanson, Philip G., & Lubin, Bernard. (1988). Team building as group development. In W. Brendan Reddy with Kaleel Jamison (Eds.), *Team building*, pp. 76-87. Alexandria, VA: NTL Institute for Applied Behavioral Science. San Diego: University Associates.

Hare, A. Paul. (1968). Phases in the development of the Bicol Development Planning Board. In Stephen Wells & A. Paul Hare (Eds.), *Studies in regional development*, pp. 29-64. Legazpi, Philippines: Bicol Development Planning Board.

————. (1972). Four dimensions of interpersonal behavior. *Psychological Reports, 30*, 499-512.

————. (1973). Theories of group development and categories for interaction analysis. *Small Group Behavior, 4*(3), 259-304.

————. (1974). Rafting across the Atlantic: Social science adrift. Paper presented at meetings of Association for Sociology in Southern Africa, Durban, July.

————. (1976). *Handbook of small group research* (2nd ed.). New York: Free Press.

————. (1980). Consensus versus majority vote: A laboratory experiment. *Small Group Behavior, 11*(2), 131-143.

————. (1982). *Creativity in small groups.* Beverly Hills, CA: Sage.

————. (1983a). A functional interpretation of interaction. In Herbert H. Blumberg et al. (Eds.), *Small groups and social interaction*, Vol. 2, pp. 429-447. Chichester, UK: Wiley.

————. (Ed.). (1983b). *The struggle for democracy in South Africa: Conflict and conflict resolution.* Cape Town, South Africa: Centre for Intergroup Studies, University of Cape Town.

————. (1985a). Creativity and conformity during Egypt-Israel cease-fire negotiations. *International Journal of Small Group Research, 1*(2), 122-130.

————. (1985b). *Social interaction as drama: Applications from conflict resolution.* Beverly Hills, CA: Sage.

————. (1986a). Conformity and creativity in negotiations: Israeli-Egyptian examples. *Israel Social Science Research, 4*(2), 21-33.

————. (1986b). Expressive and anticonforming behavior and subgroup formation on the raft Acali. *International Journal of Small Group Research*, *2*(2), 197-209.

————. (1989a). New field theory: SYMLOG research, 1960-1988. *Advances in Group Processes*, *6*, 229-257.

————. (1989b). Pre-negotiation as a type of consensus building: Old experience in a new form. Paper presented at meetings of International Society for Political Psychology, Tel Aviv.

Hare, A. Paul, & Blumberg, Herbert H. (Eds.). (1977). *Liberation without violence: A third party approach*. London: Rex Collings.

Hare, A. Paul, Blumberg, Herbert H., et al. (1988). *Dramaturgical analysis of social interaction*. New York: Praeger.

Hare, A. Paul, Blumberg, Herbert H., Davies, Martin F., & Kent, M. Valerie. (1992). *Small group research: A handbook*. Norwood, NJ: ABLEX.

Hare, A. Paul, & Mueller, John. (1979). Categories for exchange analysis in small groups: With an illustration from group psychotherapy. *Sociological Inquiry*, *49*(1), 57-64.

Hare, A. Paul, & Naveh, David. (1985). Creative problem solving: Camp David Summit, 1978. *Small Group Behavior*, *16*(2), 123-138.

————. (1986). Conformity and creativity: Camp David, 1978. *Small Group Behavior*, *17*(3), 243-268.

Hatfield, Elaine. (1983). Equity theory and research: An overview. In Herbert H. Blumberg et al. (Eds.), *Small groups and social interaction*, Vol. 2, pp. 401-411. Chichester, UK: Wiley.

Hennefrund, William. (1985). The fine art of team building. *Association Management*, *37*(8), 98-101.

Heyerdahl, Thor. (1972). *The RA expeditions*. New York: New American Library.

Hill, Gayle W. (1982). Group versus individual performance: Are N + 1 heads better than one? *Psychological Bulletin*, *91*, 517-539.

Homans, George C. (1974). *Social behavior: Its elementary forms*. New York: Harcourt Brace Jovanovich.

Horwitz, John J. (1970). *Team practice and the specialist: An introduction to interdisciplinary team work*. Springfield, IL: Charles C. Thomas.

Inglesby, Tom. (1989). Learning management from the Japanese: An interview with Kiyoshi Suzaki. *Manufacturing Systems*, *7*(6), 53-56.

International Labour Office. (1980). *Conciliation and arbitration procedures in labour disputes*. Geneva: International Labour Organization.

International Peace Academy. (1978). *Peacekeeper's handbook*. New York: International Peace Academy.

Isenberg, Daniel J. (1986). Group polarization: A critical review and meta-analysis. *Journal of Personality and Social Psychology*, *50*, 1141-1151.

Jackson, E. (1983). *Middle East mission*. New York: Norton.

Jacobs, R. C., & Everett, J. G. (1988). The importance of team building in a high-tech environment. *Journal of European Industrial Training*, *12*(4), 10-16.

Jahoda, Marie. (1956). Psychological issues in civil liberties. *American Psychologist*, *11*, 234-240.

Janis, Irving L. (1982). *Groupthink: Psychological studies of policy decisions and fiascos*. Boston: Houghton Mifflin.

Johnson, Cynthia Reedy. (1986). An outline for team building. *Training*, *23*(1), 48-52.

Kanter, Rosabeth Moss. (1983). *The change masters: Innovations for productivity in the American corporation.* New York: Simon & Schuster.

Kaplan, Martin F. (1989). Task, situational, and personal determinants of influence process in group decision making. *Advances in Group Processes*, *6*, 87-105.

Katz, Daniel, & Kahn, Robert L. (1978). *The social psychology of organizations* (2nd ed.). New York: Wiley.

Kazemek, Edward A., & Albert, Bruce M. (1988). Learning the secret to teamwork. *Healthcare Financial Management*, *42*(9), 108, 110.

Kelman, Herbert C. (1958). Compliance, identification, and internalization: Three processes of attitude change. *Journal of Conflict Resolution*, *2*, 51-60.

_____. (1987). The political psychology of the Israeli-Palestinian conflict: How can we overcome the barriers to a negotiated solution. *Political Psychology*, *8*, 347-363.

Kelman, Herbert C., & Cohen, Stephen P. (1979). The problem-solving workshop: A social-psychological contribution to the resolution of international conflicts. *Journal of Peace Research*, *13*(2), 79-90.

Kew, Francis. (1987). Contested rules: An explanation of how games change. *International Review for the Sociology of Sport*, *22*(2), 125-135.

Kiesler, Charles A. (1969). Group pressure and conformity. In Judson Mills (Ed.), *Experimental Social Psychology*, pp. 233-306. New York: Macmillan.

_____. (1971). *The psychology of commitment: Experiments linking behavior to belief.* New York: Academic Press.

Kiesler, Charles A., & Corbin, Lee H. (1965). Commitment, attraction, and conformity. *Journal of Personality and Social Psychology*, *2*, 890-895.

Kiesler, Charles A., Zanna, Mark, & de Salvo, James. (1966). Deviation and conformity: Opinion change as a function of commitment, attraction, and presence of a deviate. *Journal of Personality and Social Psychology*, *3*, 458-467.

Kissinger, Henry. (1982). *Years of upheaval.* London: Wiedenfeld & Nicholson & Michael Joseph.

Koehler, Kenneth G. (1989). Effective team management. *Small Business Reports*, *14*(7), 14-16.

Kolb, Deborah M. (1983). Strategy and tactics of mediation. *Human Relations*, *36*(3), 247-268.

Kosower, Evie. (1987). The Shokuba development program: Japan's step beyond quality circles. *Organization Development Journal*, *5*(3), 18-21.

Kouzes, James M., & Posner, Barry Z. (1988). *Leadership practices inventory (LPI).* San Diego: University Associates.

Kressel, Gideon M. (1982). *Blood feuds among urban Bedouins.* Jerusalem: Magnes Press.

LaFauci, Horatio M., & Richter, Peyton E. (1970). *Team teaching at the college level.* New York: Pergamon Press.

Larson, Carl E., & LaFasto, Frank M. J. (1989). *Team work: What must go right, what can go wrong.* Newbury Park, CA: Sage.

Latané, Bibb, Williams, Kipling, & Harkins, Stephen. (1979). Social loafing. *Psychology Today*, *13*(4): 104-110.

Lau, Barbara. (1988a). Reducing job stress through team building and positive management. *Management Quarterly, 29*(3), 26-29.

———. (1988b). Reducing job stress through team building and positive management: Part II. *Management Quarterly, 29*(4), 13-16.

Laughlin, Patrick R., & Futoran, Gail C. (1985). Collective induction: Social combination and sequential transition. *Journal of Personality and Social Psychology, 48*, 608-613.

Leavitt, Harold J. (1972). *Managerial psychology: An introduction to individuals, pairs, and groups in organizations* (3rd ed.). Chicago: University of Chicago Press.

Lee, Chris. (1989). Can leadership be taught? *Training*, July, 19-26.

Leet-Pellegrini, Helena, & Rubin, Jeffrey Z. (1974). The effects of six bases of power upon compliance, identification, and internalization. *Bulletin of the Psychonomic Society, 3*(1B, January), 68-70.

Lefton, Robert E. (1988). The eight barriers to teamwork. *Personnel Journal, 67*(1), 18-24.

Lifton, Robert L. (1961). *Thought reform and the psychology of totalism.* New York: Gollancz.

Likert, Rensis. (1967). *The human organization.* New York: McGraw-Hill.

Longabaugh, Richard. (1963). A category system for coding interpersonal behavior as social exchange. *Sociometry, 26*(3), 319-344.

Looram, James. (1985). The transition meeting: Taking over a new management team. *Supervisory Management, 30*(9), 29-36.

Loubser, Jan J., Baum, Rainer C., Effrat, Andrew, & Lidz, Victor M. (Eds.). (1976). *Explorations in general theory in social science: Essays in honor of Talcott Parsons*, Vols. I & II. New York: Free Press.

Marrow, Alfred J., Bowers, Davis G., & Seashore, Stanley E. (1967). *Management by participation: Creating a climate for personal and organizational development.* New York: Harper & Row.

Mathews, M. J., & Vogt, Judy. (1987). Effective consultant/client interaction requires teamwork, trust. *Data Management, 25*(7), 23-28.

McClelland, David. (1961). *The achieving society.* Princeton, NJ: Van Nostrand.

McDonald, John W., Jr. (1989). Paper presented at meetings of International Studies Association, London.

McGowan, Donald E., & Norton, William W. (1989). Safety—A health service team approach. *Professional Safety, 34*(1), 21-26.

McGrath, Joseph E. (1984). *Groups: Interaction and performance.* Englewood Cliffs, NJ: Prentice-Hall.

McGrath, Joseph E., & Kravitz, David A. (1982). Group research. *Annual Review of Psychology, 33*, 195-230.

McGregor, Douglas. (1960). *The human side of enterprise.* New York: McGraw-Hill.

Merritt, Sandy (Ed.). (1987). *Speaking of peace: Exploring nonviolence and conflict resolution.* London: Quaker Peace & Service.

Milgram, Stanley. (1963). Behavioral study of obedience. *Journal of Abnormal and Social Psychology, 67*(4), 371-378.

Miller, Barry W., & Phillips, Ronald C. (1986). Team building on a deadline. *Training & Development Journal, 40*(3), 54-57.

Miller, Frederick A. (1988). Moving a team to multiculturalism. In W. Brendan

Reddy with Kaleel Jamison (Eds.), *Team building*, pp. 192-197. Alexandria, VA: NTL Institute for Applied Behavioral Science. San Diego: University Associates.

Mills, Theodore M. (1964). *Group transformation*. Englewood Cliffs, NJ: Prentice-Hall.

Miskin, Val D., & Gmelch, Walter H. (1985). Quality leadership for quality teams. *Training & Development Journal*, *39*(5), 122-129.

Mitchell, Rex. (1986). Team building by disclosure of internal frames of reference. *Journal of Applied Behavioral Science*, *22*(1), 15-28.

Montville, Joseph V. (1987). The arrow and the olive branch: A case for track two diplomacy. In John W. McDonald, Jr. & Diane B. Bendahmane (Eds.), *Conflict resolution: Track two diplomacy*, pp. 5-20. Washington, D.C.: Foreign Service Institute, U.S. Department of State.

Moosbruker, Jane. (1988). Developing a productivity team: Making groups at work work. In W. Brendan Reddy with Kaleel Jamison (Eds.), *Team building*, pp. 88-97. Alexandria, VA: NTL Institute for Applied Behavioral Science. San Diego: University Associates.

Morley, Ian E., & Stephenson, Geoffrey M. (1977). *The social psychology of bargaining*. London: Allen & Unwin.

Moreno, Jacob L. (1953). *Who shall survive: foundations of sociometry, group psychotherapy, and sociodrama* (rev. ed.). Beacon, NY: Beacon House.

Moskal, Brian S. (1987). Glasnost in Dearborn. *Industry Week*, September 21, 53-55.

Mumford, Michael D., & Gustafson, Sigrid B. (1988). Creativity syndrome: integration, application, and innovation. *Psychological Bulletin*, *103*(1), 27-43.

Nanda, Ravinder. (1986). Training in team and consensus building. *Management Solutions*, *31*(9), 31-36.

Oliver, Neil, & Langford, John. (1987). Safety in team building—The contracting process. *Industrial & Commercial Training*, *19*(5), 3-5.

Olmsted, Michael S. (1959). *The small group*. New York: Random House.

Olmsted, Michael S., & Hare, A. Paul. (1978). *The small group* (2nd ed.). New York: Random House.

Orpen, Christopher. (1986). Improving organizations through team development. *Management & Labour Studies*, *11*(1), 1-12.

Owens, Thomas. (1989). Business teams. *Small Business Reports*, *14*(1), 52-58.

Palmer, Judith D. (1988). For the manager who must build a team. In W. Brendan Reddy with Kaleel Jamison (Eds.), *Team building*, pp. 137-149. Alexandria, VA: NTL Institute for Applied Behavioral Science. San Diego: University Associates.

Parnell, E. M. (1987). Self-examination—The Achilles' heel of teams. *Supervision*, *49*(2), 6-8.

Parsons, Talcott. (1961). An outline of the social system. In Talcott Parsons et al. (Eds.), *Theories of society*, pp. 30-79. New York: Free Press.

Pati, Gopal C., Salitore, Robert, & Brady, Sandra. (1987). What went wrong with quality circles. *Personnel Journal*, *66*(12), 83-87.

Patten, Thomas H., Jr. (1981). *Organizational development through teambuilding*. New York: Wiley.

———. (1988a). Team building, Part I: Designing the intervention. In W. Brendan Reddy with Kaleel Jamison (Eds.), *Team building*, pp. 15-24. Alexandria,

VA: NTL Institute for Applied Behavioral Science. San Diego: University Associates.

————. (1988b). Team building, Part II: Conducting the intervention. In W. Brendan Reddy with Kaleel Jamison (Eds.), *Team building*, pp. 25-31. Alexandria, VA: NTL Institute for Applied Behavioral Science. San Diego: University Associates.

Payne, Malcolm. (1979). *Power, authority and responsibility in social services: Socialwork in area teams.* London: Macmillan.

Peabody, Dean, & Goldberg, Lewis R. (1989). Some determinants of factor structures from personality-trait descriptors. *Journal of Personality and Social Psychology, 57*(3), 552-567.

Pearce, John A., & Ravlin, Elizabeth C. (1987). The design and activation of self-regulating work groups. *Human Relations, 40*(11), 751-782.

Phillips, Steven L., & Elledge, Robin L. (1989). *The team-building source book.* San Diego: University Associates.

Polley, Richard B., Hare, A. Paul, & Stone, Philip J. (Eds.). (1988). *The SYMLOG practitioner.* New York: Praeger.

Polti, Georges. (1977). *The thirty-six dramatic situations.* Boston: Writer.

Pritchard, Robert D., Jones, Steven D., Roth, Philip L., Stuebing, Karla, & Ekeberg, Steven E. (1988). Effects of group feedback, goal setting and incentives on organizational productivity. *Journal of Applied Psychology, 73*(2), 337-358.

Pruitt, Dean G. (1983). Achieving integrative agreements. In Max H. Bazerman & Roy J. Lewicki (Eds.), *Negotiating in organizations*, pp. 35-50. Beverly Hills, CA: Sage.

Reddy, W. Brendan, & Burke, Carol. (1988). What to look for when selecting a team building consultant: Multicultural and other considerations. In W. Brendan Reddy with Kaleel Jamison (Eds.), *Team building*, pp. 179-186. Alexandria, VA: NTL Institute for Applied Behavioral Science. San Diego: University Associates.

Reddy, W. Brendan, with Jamison, Kaleel (Eds.). (1988). *Team building: Blueprints for productivity and satisfaction.* Alexandria, VA: NTL Institute for Applied Behavioral Science. San Diego: University Associates.

Rigby, J. Malcolm. (1987). The challenge of multinational team development. *Journal of Management Development, 6*(3), 65-72.

Rohrbaugh, John. (1981). Improving the quality of group judgement: Social judgement analysis and the nominal group technique. *Organizational Behavior and Human Performance, 28*, 272-288.

Rosen, Lawrence. (1984). *Bargaining for reality.* Chicago: University of Chicago Press.

Rosenbaum, Milton E., Moore, Danny L., Cotton, John L., Cook, Michael S., Hieser, Rex A., Shovar, M. Nicki, & Gray, Morris J. (1980). Group productivity and process: Pure and mixed reward structures and task interdependence. *Journal of Personality and Social Psychology, 39*, 626-42.

Roth, Bill. (1989). Just starting or extending your process? Five phases to success. *Journal for Quality & Participation*, June, 26-32.

Rothman, Jay. (1989). Developing pre-negotiation theory and practice. Jerusalem: Leonard Davis Institute for International Relations, Hebrew University, Policy paper.

Scher, Jordan M. (1974). Conflict, negotiation, and cooperation: An analysis of these parameters in national and international relations. *American Journal of Psychotherapy, 28*(2), 222-234.

Schindler-Rainman, Eva. (1988). Team building in voluntary organizations. In W. Brendan Reddy with Kaleel Jamison (Eds.), *Team building*, pp. 119-123. Alexandria, VA: NTL Institute for Applied Behavioral Science. San Diego: University Associates.

Schmuck, Richard, Runkel, Philip, & Langmeyer, Daniel. (1971). Theory to guide organizational training in schools. *Sociological Inquiry, 41*(2), 183-191.

Schutz, William C. (1958). *FIRO: A three-dimensional theory of interpersonal behavior.* New York: Holt, Rinehart.

Sedel, Rae. (1989). HR implications of the European unification. *Personnel, 66*(10), 18-24.

Shambaugh, Philip W. (1978). The development of the small group. *Human Relations, 31*(3), 283-295.

Shaplin, Judson T. (1964). Toward a theoretical rationale for team teaching. In Judson T. Shaplin & Henry F. Olds, Jr. (Eds.), *Team teaching*, pp. 57-98. New York: Harper & Row.

Shaplin, Judson T., & Olds, Henry F., Jr. (Eds.). (1964). *Team teaching.* New York: Harper & Row.

Shaw, Marvin E. (1981). *Group dynamics* (3rd ed.). New York: McGraw-Hill.

Sherif, Muzafer. (1935). A study of some factors in perception. *Archives of Psychology, 27* (187).

Silver, Steven D., Cohen, Bernard P., & Rainwater, Julie. (1988). Group structure and information exchange in innovative problem solving. *Advances in Group Processes,* 25, 169-194.

Simpson, J. C., & Weiner, E.S.C. (Comps.). (1989). *The Oxford English dictionary* (2nd ed.). Oxford: Clarendon Press.

Stein, Janice Gross. (1988). Getting to the table: Triggers, stages, functions, and consequences of prenegotiation. Toronto: Department of Political Science, University of Toronto.

Stein, Morris I. (1974). *Stimulating creativity: Individual procedures*, Vol. 1. New York: Academic Press.

_____. (1975). *Stimulating creativity: Group procedures*, Vol. 2. New York: Academic Press.

Steiner, Gary Albert (Ed.). (1965). *The creative organization.* Chicago: University of Chicago Press.

Steiner, Ivan D. (1972). *Group process and productivity.* New York: Academic Press.

Stock, Dorothy, & Thelen, Herbert A. (1958). *Emotional dynamics and group culture: Experimental studies of individual and group behavior.* New York: New York University Press.

Stogdill, Ralph M. (1974). *Handbook of leadership: A survey of theory and research.* New York: Free Press.

Street, Warren R. (1974). Brainstorming by individuals, coacting and interacting groups. *Journal of Applied Psychology, 59,* 433-436.

Sundstrom, Eric, & Altman, Irwin. (1989). Physical environments and work-group effectiveness. *Research in Organizational Behavior, 11,* 175-209.

Sundstrom, Eric, DeMeuse, Kenneth P., & Futrell, David. (1990). Work teams: Applications and effectiveness. *American Psychologist, 45*(2), 120-133.

Taylor, Irving A. (1975). An emerging view of creative actions. In Irving A. Taylor

& Jacob W. Getzels (Eds.), *Perspectives in creativity*, pp. 297-325. Chicago: Aldine.

Thelen, Herbert A. (1949). Group dynamics in instruction: Principle of least group size. *School Review, 57*, 139-148.

Thibaut, John W., & Kelley, Harold H. (1959). *The social psychology of groups.* New York: Wiley.

_____. (1986). *Social psychology of groups* (Rev. ed.). New Brunswick, NJ: Transaction Books.

Tindale, R. Scott, & Davis, James H. (1985). Individual and group reward allocation decisions in two situational contexts: Effects of relative need and performance. *Journal of Personality and Social Psychology, 48*, 1148-1161.

Tolle, Ernest F. (1988). Management team building: Yes but! *Engineering Management International, 4*(4), 277-285.

Touval, Saadia. (1982). *The peace brokers: Mediators in the Arab-Israeli conflict.* Princeton, NJ: Princeton University Press.

Tuckman, Bruce W. (1965). Developmental sequence in small groups. *Psychological Bulletin, 63*(6), 384-399.

Tuckman, Bruce W., & Jensen, Mary A. (1977). Stages of small-group development revisited. *Group and Organization Studies, 2*(4), 419-427.

Turner, Jonathan H. (1989). A theory of microdynamics. *Advances in Group Processes, 6*, 1-26.

Ulschak, Francis L., Nathanson, Leslie, & Gillan, Peter G. (1981). *Small group problem solving: An aid to organizational effectiveness.* Reading, MA: Addison-Wesley.

Wall, James A. (1981). Mediation: An analysis, review, and proposed research. *Journal of Conflict Resolution, 25*(1), 157-180.

Walton, Richard E. (1969). *Interpersonal peacemaking.* Reading, MA: Addison-Wesley.

Weisbord, Marvin R. (1985). Team effectiveness theory. *Training & Development Journal, 39*(1), 27-29.

_____. (1988). Team work: Building productive relationships. In W. Brendan Reddy with Kaleel Jamison (Eds.), *Team building*, pp. 35-44. Alexandria, VA: NTL Institute for Applied Behavioral Science. San Diego: University Associates.

Whatley, Arthur A., & Hoffman, Wilma. (1987). Quality circles earn union respect. *Personnel Journal, 66*(11), 89-93.

Wolff, Michael F. (1988). Before you try team building. *Research-Technology Management., 31*(1), 6-8.

Wolpert, Lewis, & Richards, Alison. (1988). *A passion for science.* Oxford: Oxford University Press.

Woodcock, Mike, & Francis, Dave. (1980). Team building: Yes or no? in William W. Burke & Leonard D. Goodstein (Eds.), *Trends and issues in OD: Current theory and practice*, pp. 185-198. San Diego: University Associates.

Woodman, Richard W., & Sherwood, John J. (1980a). Effects of team development intervention: A field experiment. *Journal of Applied Behavioral Science, 16*(2), 211-227.

_____. (1980b). The role of team development in organizational effectiveness: A critical review. *Psychological Bulletin, 88*(1), 166-186.

Worrall, P., Mitson, R., Dorrance, E. B., Williams, R. J., & Frame, J.W.N. (1970).

Teaching from strength: An introduction to team teaching. London: Hamish Hamilton.

Yetton, Philip, & Bottger, Preston. (1983). The relationships among group size, member ability, social decision schemes, and performance. *Organizational Behavior and Human Performance, 32,* 145-159.

Zager, Robert, & Rosow, Michael P. (1982). *The innovative organization: Productivity programs in action.* New York: Pergamon Press.

Zajonc, Robert B. (1965). Social facilitation. *Science, 149,* 269-274.

Zander, Alvin. (1977). *Groups at work.* San Francisco: Jossey-Bass.

Name Index

Subject Index

ABOUT THE AUTHOR

A. PAUL HARE is Professor of Sociology at Ben-Gurion University of the Negev in Israel. From 1973 to 1980, he was Professor of Sociology at the University of Cape Town in South Africa, and before that he taught at Haverford and Harvard. He is the author of *Handbook of Small Group Research* (1962), *The Small Group*, with M. Olmsted (1978), *Creativity in Small Groups* (1982), *Social Interaction as Drama* (1985), *Dramaturgical Analysis of Social Interaction*, with H. Blumberg (Praeger, 1988), and *Small Group Research*, with H. Blumberg, M. Davies, and M. V. Kent (1992). He is also the co-editor of nine other books and the author of numerous journal articles.